SRI LANKAN
COOKING

64 Fabulous Recipes from the Chefs and Kitchens of Sri Lanka

**Douglas Bullis &
Wendy Hutton**
Photos by **Luca Invernizzi Tettoni**

TUTTLE Publishing
Tokyo | Rutland, Vermont | Singapore

CONTENTS

Food in Sri Lanka

Cinnamon, cloves and other spices are the island's culinary gems

Sri Lanka, the fabled island of sapphires, rubies and other precious stones, is home to one of the least known Asian cuisines. Rarely found in restaurants outside the island itself, Sri Lankan fare is often mistaken for yet another Indian regional cuisine. To the culinary explorer, however, Sri Lankan food is as intriguing and unique as the many other customs of this island paradise.

Sri Lanka, formerly known as Ceylon, is located off India's southeast coast. The rugged terrain of the central highlands—characterised by high mountains and plateaus, steep river gorges and swathes of tea plantations—dominates much of the island. This falls away to sandy lowlands, rice paddies and long stretches of palm-fringed beaches.

The ancestors of today's Sinhalese people arrived some 2,500 years ago from Northern India. They named themselves after a mythic ancestor who was born of a *sinha* (lion) and a princess. After conquering the local Yakshas, a succession of kingdoms—Sinhalese in the centre and south, and Tamil in the Jaffna Peninsula—rose and fell over the centuries. The first Portuguese ships chanced upon Sri Lanka in the early sixteenth century and set about trading in cinnamon and other spices. There followed four hundred years of Western presence in the form of Portuguese, Dutch and finally the British before Sri Lanka regained her independence in 1948.

Such diverse influences may be tasted in dishes of Arab *biryani* (yellow rice with meat and nuts), Malay *nasi kuning* (turmeric rice), Portuguese semolina love cakes, and Dutch *breuders* (dough cakes) and *lampries* (savoury rice and meat packets).

Sri Lankan cuisine, which is based upon rice with vegetable, fish or meat curries, and a variety of side dishes and condiments, reflects the geographical and ethnic differences of the land. Seafood dishes, such as Spicy Fish Stew (*seer* fish stew), Tamarind Claypot Fish (*ambulthiyal*), Coconut Curry Crabs and Rich Seafood Soup (Jaffna *kool*), are common to coastal and, increasingly, inland areas. The eating of large animals, such as cows and deer, is less popular due to the predominantly Buddhist and Hindu population; chicken and freshwater fish are usually preferred instead.

Sri Lanka is also blessed with an abundant harvest of fruits and vegetables. Jackfruit, breadfruit, okra, gourds, plantains and drumsticks are but some of the vegetables, tubers, and leaves that feature in one or other Sri Lankan dish.

It is a cuisine expressed in spices—cinnamon, cloves, nutmeg, coriander, mace, pepper, cardamom, red chillies, mustard seeds, cumin, fenugreek and turmeric are all used to flavour curries, while some add flavour to desserts and cakes. The spices of Sri Lanka, which helped to shape the history of the island, are truly its culinary gems.

A Gustatory Paradise

Sri Lanka's dry and wet seasons are reversed from one side of the island to the other by two monsoons. From May to August, the southwest monsoon, Yala, brings heavy rain to the southern, western and central highland regions, leaving the other side dry. From October to January, the gentler northeast monsoon, Maha, brings rain to the north of the island. The coastal regions are hot and humid year round, while the hill country feels like perpetual spring.

When Sri Lanka's first settlers arrived from India in about 500 BC, the coastal lowlands they found were no paradise. Undaunted, they set to work making them one. They had brought with them the techniques of turning a stream into a small pond, and of digging sluices with gates to let water into small fields on demand. What happened over the next ten centuries is one of the greatest irrigation feats in world history:

TOP, FROM LEFT Cinnamon, cloves, nutmeg, coriander seeds, mace, pepper and cardamon pods.

BOTTOM, FROM LEFT Turmeric, fennel, fenugreek, cumin, mustard seeds and dried red chillies.

Sri Lanka's system of reservoir "tanks" feeding a latticework of watercourses produced a rice surplus so large that it financed the island's architectural and sculptural splendours.

The simple brown rice of those early times became the twenty-odd varieties grown today. The two monsoons translate to two harvests a year over much of the island. Low-country rice is mostly plain white rice that cooks easily and has no strong taste to distract from the curries. Somewhat upscale is a red rice that bursts as it cooks, yielding a fluffy white interior with reddish flecks on the surface—this is the festive *suduru samba* served when entertaining guests. The highest grade of rice is long-grained basmati, often used when aromatic dishes are desired. In between, many lesser varieties are grown, usually in small quantities for local use.

However, paddy agriculture is far from the only kind of farming. Slash-and-burn, or *chena* farming, is the bane of the back country, as it produces only two or three harvests of millet and root vegetables before depleting the soils and forcing the farmer to move on. But for many poor people, it is the only choice.

In a category all of its own is the island's enormous production of tea. The nuances of Sri Lankan tea are as complex and sophisticated as the nuances of fine wine. Small family plantations can be found even a few kilometres inland from the coast, but the higher the plantation the better the tea. The premium Dambula and other highland teas grow on tidily pruned plantations that undulate over the landscape as gracefully as slow-flowing water. The teas are processed in multi-storey factories painted white or silver that stand out amid the landscape like ghosts on a green sea.

And of course one can't overlook the island's spice gardens. The gaily proclaimed ones along the highways to Kandy are for tourists. The serious spice plantations growing for export are found in moist valleys or hilly areas. Be they for tourist or export, the goods are the same: over here spindly, weedy bushes whose flower yields a darkish nubbin that dries into clove; over there bushy nutmeg trees with bright tan fruit.

The delicate seed pods of the cardamom grow symbiotically under clove plants. Gangly peppercorns cluster under the long leaves of their plant, looking rather like grape bunches that took their diet too seriously. Visitors to these professional spiceries are treated to a fabulous bouquet of odours as they learn all about how spices are grown and prepared for consumers the world over.

A final glance at the country's agriculture focuses on the men who walk ropeways high in the sky doing the dangerous job of harvesting drippings from the flowers of the *kitul* palm. Treading gingerly along a single rope and guyline 15 metres (50 feet) or more above the ground, they tie shut the tips of the *kitul's* flowers with cord so they cannot open. The sap, which ordinarily would go into swelling the flower and then filling its fruit, instead oozes into clay pots tied to the flower's stem. Every few days these are visited by the tappers, who empty the juice into a pot slung around their waists.

The resulting treacle has a unique flavour which matches superbly with Sri Lanka's high-butterfat but bland curd or buffalo-milk yoghurt. When the treacle is hardened by boiling and then cooled, it becomes jaggery, the most popular sweetener on the island and an essential ingredient in most Sri Lankan desserts and sweetmeats.

A close cousin of this process does the same with coconut flowers. The frothy white sap ferments into toddy or *ra*, a foamy white alcohol that can be drunk as is or distilled into arrack.

LEFT Wall painting at Sigiriya.

OPPOSITE Fruit vendors pile their stalls high with whichever fruits are in season.

Ra is such a staple that it even lent its name to a town on the Colombo– Kandy railway line, Ragama—literally "Toddy Town."

The sea's bounty includes several kinds of tuna, plus grouper, whitefish, kingfish, barracuda, trevally, squid, octopus and a host of lesser species. One of the most popular fish in Sri Lanka is the seer or Spanish mackerel which is cooked in many styles.

Most fishing is done from old-fashioned *oruwa* dugout outrigger canoes lashed together with coconut-fibre twine. The old handmade *katta maran* (literally "big logs" and the origin of the word "catamaran") dugouts come in various hues of salt-toughened wood. Their crews divide between "netters" and "chummers," the latter a term for hook-and-line fishers that was borrowed from the British.

The fish left over after those for household use are sold to itinerant hawkers who have mounted wide wooden boxes on the back of bicycles. They wobble their way into the countryside, fish tails sticking out either side of the box, calling out "Lu! Lu!" (short for *malu*, the Sinhalese word for fish).

A drive along the coastal highway passes one ramshackle wooden roadside stall after the other with gorgeous rows of tuna lined up like cordwood. They also sell squid, *seer*, kingfish, slabs of shark big enough to cover a dinner plate, and tiny silver sprats that are dried and munched like popcorn.

Other stalls display freshly caught skipjacks drying in the sun. Although the chewy locally-dried tuna is often referred to as "Maldive fish," the authentic Maldive fish used in restaurants is tougher than dried leather.

The most idiosyncratic of Sri Lanka's fishermen are the island's famous stilt fishers. These men wedge sturdy poles into rock crevices in the shallows, to which they attach a tiny sling-net that passes for a seat. While the catch is modest, some of the brilliantly coloured coral-dwellers they bring in, such as the striped mullet, are among the tastiest on the island.

Another fishing style is net casting. Fishermen patrol tidal pools and rocky ledges in the late afternoon in search of the parrotfish or trevally hungry enough to let down its guard as night approaches. Netters have hurling styles so unique that locals can identify someone at a distance by the way he throws his net.

— **Douglas Bullis**

One Land, Many Cuisines

Sri Lanka's multi-ethnic population ensures culinary variety

Sri Lanka boasts a vast array of tropical fruits, vegetables and spices, as well as an abundance of fish and other seafood in its lakes, rivers and seas, and wild game in its forests. The way Sri Lankans put this bounty together in the kitchen depends to some extent on where they live, and even more upon their ethnic and religious background.

The multi-ethnic mix of people living on this small island comprises Sinhalese, Tamils, Moors (Muslims), Burghers and Eurasians, Malays and Veddhas.

The majority of the population are Sinhalese, believed to be descended from Indo-Aryans who arrived from northern India more than 2,000 years ago and intermarried with scattered groups of tribal Veddhas. Over the centuries, the cooking of the Sinhalese has evolved into two slightly different styles: coastal or "low country" Sinhalese, and Kandy or "upcountry" Sinhalese.

Regardless of where they live, the staple food for Sinhalese (and indeed, for all Sri Lankans) is rice. This is usually accompanied by a range of spiced vegetables, fish, poultry, meat or game dishes. Most Sinhalese are Buddhist and although the taking of life is against Buddhist teachings, most Sinhalese don't mind eating food which has been killed by others. Strict Buddhists, however, are vegetarians (something they share with a number of Hindu Tamils).

In coastal Sinhalese cuisine, fish and other seafood feature far more widely than poultry or meat, and coconut milk is the preferred base for curries. Towns such as Bentota, Chilaw and Batticaloa are noted for excellent seafood but most famous of all is Negombo. The crab and prawn dishes from this west coast town are well-known throughout Sri Lanka. Negombo is also the site of one of the island's busiest and most colourful fish markets.

A Galle Market trader displays his *kiri peni* or curd and honey, a popular Sri Lankan snack. The "honey" that one sees in the roadside stalls and on restaurant menus is really treacle from the *kitul* palm. Curd is traditionally made from buffalo milk.

Another Sinhalese specialty from the coast is Tamarind Claypot Fish or *ambulthiyal*. At its best in the Southern town of Ambalangoda, *ambulthiyal* is a dish of *balaya* (bonito) which uses tamarind as both a flavouring and a preservative—even in Sri Lanka's heat and humidity, this dish can keep for up to a week.

An ingredient known as Maldive fish is widely used as a seasoning throughout Sri Lanka, but especially in coastal regions. It is made from a type of bonito (also known as skipjack) which is boiled, smoked and sun-dried until it is rock hard.

Kandy, the heart of upcountry Sri Lanka, remained an independent Sinhalese kingdom until the British finally took over in 1815, thus it largely escaped the social and culinary influences of the Portuguese and Dutch. Thanks to the higher altitude and cooler climate, a wide range of vegetables and fruits flourish around Kandy and other upcountry regions, which are renowned for their range of delicious vegetable dishes.

Many Kandian curries are made with unusual ingredients such as young jackfruit, jackfruit seeds, cashews, breadfruit and green papaya, while various edible flowers such as turmeric, hibiscus and sesbania may end up in an omelette or curry. Game, including deer and wild birds, was also an upcountry favourite, although dwindling forests and restrictions on hunting in protected areas have diminished the amount of game now being cooked in upcountry kitchens.

Sinhalese refer to their main meal as "rice and curry," and normally serve several types of spiced or "curried" dishes of vegetables, fish, meat or poultry. Curries are classified by their spicing and method of cooking rather than by their main ingredient. Thus, there are "red" curries which contain an often incendiary amount of chilli and usually a limited number of spices. There are also the distinctively Sinhalese "black" curries which develop a wonderfully rich aroma and flavour, thanks to the technique of roasting whole spices (primarily coriander, cumin and fennel) to a rich brown colour before grinding them.

"Brown" curries are made from unroasted spices, while "white" curries, which contain plenty of coconut milk and very little chilli, are generally quite mild.

When choosing which curries to serve with the rice, Sinhalese cooks ensure that there is a variety of textures as well as flavours, with at least one fairly liquid, or soupy, curry to help moisten the rice, and usually a relatively dry curry with a thick gravy. One of the curries will most likely be a spiced lentil dish, and there is sure to be at least one pungent side dish or condiment known as a *sambol* (from the Malay *sambal*). These *sambol*, also know as "rice pullers," are guaranteed to whet the appetite with their basic ingredient—anything from onion to bitter gourd, dried prawns to salted lime—heightened by the flavours of chilli, onion, salt and Maldive fish.

One of the most popular sambol, Fresh Coconut Sambol (*pol sambol*), is made with freshly grated coconut; a simple meal of rice, lentils, Fresh Coconut Sambol and *mallung* is inexpensive, nutritious, and utterly satisfying. *Mallung*, which provides an unmistakable Sinhalese accent to every meal, is a vitamin- and mineral-packed mixture of leafy greens, freshly grated coconut, lime juice, chilli and powdered Maldive fish. Many of the greens used in a *mallung* are plucked from the kitchen garden, including young passionfruit leaves, *gotu kala* (Asian pennywort), young chilli leaves, young leaves from the drumstick tree and the leaves of the flowering cassia tree.

The first Tamils are believed to have arrived at about the same time as the Indo-Ayrans, around 2,000 years ago. Successive waves of Tamils from southern India established themselves in Sri Lanka, mostly in

Stilt fishermen wedge wooden poles into rock crevices to use as a perch while fishing.

the north, on the Jaffna peninsula. In the mid to late nineteenth and early twentieth centuries, Tamil labourers were brought in by the British to work on the tea estates in the cooler hilly areas of Sri Lanka. These later arrivals are generally referred to as Indian Tamils, to distinguish them from the long-established Jaffna Tamils.

The majority of Sri Lanka's Tamils are Hindu, therefore they do not eat beef. Indeed, most Jaffna Tamils are strict vegetarians. Vegetables are grown in the gardens of countless families in Jaffna, irrigated by deep wells; anyone who has tasted fresh home-grown vegetables cooked Tamil style is indeed fortunate.

The Tamil dishes found in Sri Lanka are similar to those of southeast India, where the vegetarian cuisine is among the world's finest. As with Sinhalese food, the basis of Tamil food is influenced by the teachings of the Ayurveda, ancient texts on the "wisdom of life and longevity." Seasonings such as curry leaves, brown mustard seed and dried chillies are widely used, while freshly grated coconut, coconut milk and yoghurt appear in many vegetable dishes.

Popular Tamil dishes found in Sri Lanka include *rasam*, a spicy sour soup that is an aid to digestion; *kool*, a thick seafood soup originating from Jaffna fisherfolk; *vadai* or deep-fried savouries made with black gram flour; and many types of vegetable *pachadi*, where cooked vegetables are tossed with curd or yoghurt and freshly grated coconut. Dosai, slightly sour pancakes made with black gram and rice flours, constitute another delicious Tamil contribution to the culinary scene. Some Tamil dishes, such as the steamed rice-flour rolls known as *pittu*, have been adopted by Sinhalese and are now regarded as Sri Lankan.

Sri Lanka's Muslims are believed to be descended from Arab traders who settled in and around Galle, Beruwala and Puttalam from as early as the eighth century, and from Indian Muslims who migrated from southwest India.

Ingredients such as rose water, saffron (not to be confused with turmeric, which is often called "saffron" or "Indian saffron" in Sri Lanka), cashews and mint, as well as dishes like *biryani* rice, korma curries and *faluda* (a dessert of cornflour and water) all reflect Arab or Indian Muslim influence on Sri Lanka's cuisine. Arabs are also credited with planting the first coffee trees—native to the Arabian peninsula—in Sri Lanka.

In general, Muslim food is slightly sweeter than Sinhalese and Tamil food, but it certainly isn't lacking in spice. In fact, Arab traders are said to have been responsible for bringing spices such as cloves and nutmeg from the Moluccan islands to Sri Lanka long before the Dutch colonised what they called the Dutch East Indies (now Indonesia). Muslim dishes in Sri Lanka never contain pork, which is forbidden by Islam, and pork is only occasionally eaten by the Christian Tamils and Sinhalese.

In more recent times, Malays, who were brought by the Dutch, have intermarried with the Muslim community and brought with them several dishes which have since become part of the Sri Lankan kitchen. *Sathe* is the Sri Lankan equivalent of satay or cubes of meat threaded on skewers and served with a peanut and chilli sauce. Other Malay dishes include *gula melaka* (sago pudding with jaggery), *nasi kuning* (turmeric rice), *barbuth* (honeycomb tripe curry), *seenakku* and *parsong* (two types of rice flour cakes).

The multi-ethnic mix of people living on this small island has resulted in a varied and fascinating cuisine that is delicious regardless of the geographic, ethnic or religious origin.

Spice and Other Things Nice

Spices, so important to the Sri Lankan kitchen, actually helped shape the history of the island. The Portuguese arrived at the beginning of the sixteenth century and it was Sri Lanka's famous cinnamon—the delicately fragrant bark of the *Cinnamomum zeylanicum* tree

Cinnamon sticks are in fact dried curls of bark which are removed in thin slivers from the *Cinnamomum zeylanicum* tree. Cassia, which is often sold as cinnamon, comes from a related species and is darker brown in colour with a stronger flavour.

native to the island—which became the prime source of revenue for the Europeans.

Sri Lanka's cinnamon trees, which grew wild on the southern and western coasts of the island, were said to produce the finest cinnamon in the world—and sold for three times the price of cinnamon from other regions. It was said that "it healeth, it openeth and strengtheneth the mawe and digesteth the meat; it is also used against all kinde of pyson that may hurt the hart."

Cinnamon was still the most important source of revenue by the time the Dutch seized control of the island. They introduced penalties to protect it, making it a capital offence to damage a plant, and to sell or to export the quills or their oil. The Dutch did eventually succeed in cultivating cinnamon, but still relied largely on the wild supply. By the nineteenth century, however, the supremacy of cinnamon was challenged by the cheaper cassia bark grown elsewhere in Asia. The flavour is far less refined, and cassia bark lacks the faint sweetness of true cinnamon, but as the price was so competitive, Sri Lankan cinnamon eventually lost its dominance.

Cloves and nutmeg, indigenous to the Moluccas in eastern Indonesia, were planted in Sri Lanka by the Dutch who controlled most of the Dutch East Indies. Cardamom, indigenous to both Sri Lanka and southern India, was another valuable spice which flourished in the wetter regions of the country.

All of Sri Lanka's spices are used to flavour savoury dishes such as curries; some also add their fragrance and flavour to desserts and cakes. Spices such as cinnamon therefore command a very important position in Sri Lankan culture, not only as culinary flavourings but also by virtue of their having played such a major role in the country's history.

— Wendy Hutton

Colonial Tastes

Portuguese, Dutch and British influences and the creation of a Burgher culture

British colonials celebrate the end of World War II with a victory dinner in Colombo.

The wave of Western expansionism which began at the end of the fifteenth century, when the Portuguese first rounded the Cape of Good Hope and reached the west coast of India, was to have a significant impact on Sri Lanka. Over the next four centuries, colonialism affected not only the agriculture, social structure and religions of the country, but also the cuisine.

In fact, it was cuisine that attracted the Portuguese in the first place, or to be more precise, spices. With refrigeration and modern methods of food preservation, it is difficult today to imagine how vital and valuable spices were several centuries ago. They were used to help preserve food and also to mask the flavours of food that might not necessarily be in prime condition. Many spices have medicinal properties and some were believed to ward off the plagues that frequently swept through Europe.

The trade in spices—particularly pepper, nutmeg, cloves, cinnamon and cardamom—was then controlled by Arab merchants, who obtained the spices in various parts of Asia and then sold them to Venetian merchants at exorbitant prices. The search for the source of these valuable spices prompted the Portuguese to set out on their voyages of exploration. Not only did they intend to cut out the Arab middlemen, they were also filled with missionary zeal, intent on obtaining Christian converts.

By the early 1600s, the Portuguese had gained control of the southwest coast of Sri Lanka (which they called Zeilan) and had converted some of the Sinhalese royalty to Catholicism. The island was an important source of revenue, thanks to its spices (particularly cinnamon), and was also an ideal place for Portuguese vessels to take on supplies in their voyages between their colonies of Goa and Malacca.

The Portuguese introduced a number of plants they had discovered in the Americas, the most important being chilli, as well as corn, tomatoes and guavas. It is hard to imagine Sri Lankan cuisine without chilli, but prior to the introduction of this taste-tingling plant, all Asians had to rely on pepper for heat. The Portuguese impact on the cuisine of Sri Lanka has lasted until today, but almost exclusively in the area of rich cakes: *bolo de coco* (a coconut cake), *foguete* (deep-fried pastry tubes with a sweet filling) and *bolo folhadao* (a layered cake) are all a legacy of the Portuguese.

By the end of the seventeenth century, the people of Sri Lanka were desperate to oust the Portuguese; they promised the Dutch the monopoly of the rich spice trade if they could get rid of these foreigners who "never took pains to find out what the local laws and customs were." However, it proved to be a matter of exchanging one colonial master for another, as the Dutch pushed the Portuguese out and then extended their control over most of the island, except for Kandy, which remained an independent Sinhalese kingdom.

The Dutch—who controlled most of the islands in the Dutch East Indies and who had followed the Portuguese as rulers of Malacca—brought in a number of Malays to Sri Lanka (there was even a Malay regiment). They also introduced several fruits indigenous to the Malay peninsula, including rambutan, mangosteen and durian, as well as Malay names for certain dishes, including spicy condiments (*sambol*) and pickles (*achchar*).

Like the Portuguese, the Dutch left a number of cakes to become part of the culinary legacy of Sri Lanka and particularly of the Burgher community, including *breudher*, a rich cake made with yeast.

Dutch meatballs or *frikadel*, appear as part of a cross-cultural dish served on special occasions in many Sri Lankan homes. *Lampries* (a corruption of the Dutch *lomprijst*) combines these meatballs with a typically Sinhalese curry made with four types of meat and a tangy *sambol*, all wrapped up in a piece of banana leaf and steamed.

Another Dutch recipe, *smore* or sliced braised beef, has evolved over the years into a version that would not be recognised in Holland, with the meat simmered in spiced coconut milk accented with tamarind juice.

By the end of the eighteenth century, the British, with their superior naval force, had started to push the Dutch out of the island they called Ceylon. However, it took almost another two decades until they managed to topple the independent kingdom of Kandy and to exert control over the entire island.

The British had by far the greatest impact of any of the colonial rulers. They abolished most of the discriminatory regulations and monopolies established by the Dutch and brought about a significant change in the island's economy. By the mid-1800s, coffee—planted in the hill country in the interior—had replaced cinnamon as the island's most valuable crop. However, a blight virtually wiped out the coffee plantations in the late 1870s.

Tea seedlings had been imported from China in 1824 and from Assam in 1839, and the first tea estates were established by 1867—just in time to take over in importance after the failure of the coffee crop. The import of large numbers of southern Indian Tamils to work on the coffee and tea estates was another move to have a significant impact on the shape of the country.

Burghers, other wealthy locals and Europeans enjoy an evening at the Orient Club in the early twentieth century.

Labourers at a spice plantation peel cinnamon bark on the verandah of the factory in 1900.

Inevitably, as there had been intermarriage between the Portuguese and Dutch and local woman, so too was there intermarriage with the British. However, one observer remarked, in the late 1870s, that the "English, Scotch or German mechanical engineer, road officer or locomotive foreman generally marries the native burgher female with whom he associates; the civil servant, merchant, planter and army officer only keeps her."

The children of these marriages became known, during the Dutch period, as Burghers or "town dwellers." This term was also used for people of Portuguese descent, and later, for those who had British blood. Christian converts were able to escape the social distinctions of the traditional caste system and the Burghers became a privileged minority. Their fluency in Dutch and later in English, ensured they found work in various government departments and even as lawyers.

The British influence on Burgher food seems to be limited to the way meals are served. In many Burgher homes, lunch is the universal "curry and rice." However, the evening meal is often served British style, in what is called a "course" dinner. This usually begins with a soup and might be followed by a spiced meat stew, potatoes or bread and vegetables. Many of these dishes are based on Dutch or British recipes, but with sufficient spices and seasonings added to please the palates of those accustomed to more flavourful Sinhalese food.

— Wendy Hutton

Banking on Tea

Or how the word "Ceylon" was immortalised

A serendipitous twist turned a disastrous blight of coffee rust, which swept through the island's coffee estates in the 1870s, into a tea bonanza: the pretty but unassuming little bush became Sri Lanka's chief export and immortalised the word "Ceylon." A few tea plants brought from China took very well to the cool, crisp highland climate of the Looloo-condrie Estate near Kandy. The island's planters were much relieved to find that tea plants love the same climate that coffee does and that tea has just as enthusiastic a following all around the world.

Converting a green leaf into a tasty brown beverage is a quite a story in inorganic chemistry. Yet it is an everyday event in the slab-sided white or aluminium-painted tea factories that dot the flowing hills. These are slatted with louvres to hasten the drying process. Within them the three steps of withering, grinding and fermenting, convert the fresh leaves to a moist, black mass which is then heated in a stove to reduce to two percent all the moisture originally contained in the leaf.

Once broken into flakes, tea is graded into names based on the size of the flake. These names have the kind of arcane character often emanating from professionals when talking to each other. In the case of tea, the size categories are pekoe, orange pekoe, broken orange pekoe, broken orange pekoe fannings, and dust—the latter a low quality, inexpensive tea that finds its way into many of the world's teabags.

The graded teas are auctioned and exported, with the buyers relying on the expertise of their own tasters to guide them. The subtle variants of flavour in the vocabulary of tea are reminiscent of the argot wine-tasters use. Expert tasters classify tea into categories such as malty, pointy, bakey, thick, coppery, dull, and bright according to strength, flavour and colour.

The hill country where the best teas are grown is perhaps the most scenic part of Sri Lanka. Miles of lush green foliage and forest undulate across the hills and pickers move among the rows like vividly coloured butterflies.

— **Douglas Bullis**

A hill country tea plantation.

Dining in Sri Lanka

From street vendors to luxury hotels, eating in Sri Lanka is feast for all the senses

Breakfast in Sri Lanka is often a batter of rice flour cooked in special hemispherical pans to make *appa* or hoppers. These are small, bowl-shaped pancakes made by pouring a thin batter into the middle of the pan, then carefully rotating it so the batter climbs further and further up the side. The result is a soft, bready centre and crisp brown edges that goes well with *kitul*-palm treacle and buffalo-milk yoghurt. Crack an egg into the middle of a hopper before turning the pan results in an egg hopper; these go best with thick, highly spiced *sambol*. Another rice-batter dish, called the "string hopper," is quite different. These are tangled little circles of steamed noodles usually served with a *hodhi* or thin curry sauce. String hoppers are jacks-of-all-trades, good any time of the day.

Sri Lankans lunch between noon and two, often with a plate of "short eats." These divide equally between crisply baked filo-dough biscuits and *frikadels* or deep-fried rolls or balls. The interiors are filled with meat, fish or vegetables. Short eats are joined by *vadai* or deep-fried donuts of lentils, spices and flour. In the island's legion of "hotels" or fast-food restaurants, short eats come to the table as a tray filled with the house specials. The bill is determined by how many are left.

Another common snack is *roti*, a square or triangular wrap of dough stuffed with fresh chillies, onions, vegetables and cooked egg, meat or fish, which is fried on a searing sheet-metal griddle over a propane burner. Ask for a *kotthu roti* and the cook will chop up the *roti* as it cooks. The result is a meal that cools quickly—perfect for people on the go.

Many prefer a rice-and-curry lunch packet. Inside a banana leaf or thin plastic wrap is a cup or two of boiled rice, a piece of curried chicken, fish or beef for non-vegetarians, or simply some curried vegetables. All this plus its *sambol* is priced so low they're the best value on the island.

Street vendors sit beside piles of orange-yellow king-coconuts. These are a variety that produces *thambli* juice, slightly sweet, aromatic, fruity and refreshing. (Green coconuts make a thicker meat layer but the juice is not so tasty.) The stall owner lops off its top with a scythe-like knife, then punches through into the interior with four quick chops until liquid spurts out. Sri Lankans simply tip it up and drink it with no glass or straw.

Evening meals at home are an exercise in the wife's formidable cooking talents. Each woman has her own spice blends for different dishes. Most women buy their spices in bulk and take just enough for a few meals to the grinding mills that dot every village and city. Rural women powder their own at home using stone mills called *kurakkan gala* (rotating mill) or *ulundu* (small mortar and pestle). A proper rice-and-curry dinner involves three or more accompaniments, at least two of them vegetables—women consider it lax to prepare them all using a single curry.

There are few native desserts but many *rasokavili* or sweets. *Kaum* (Topknot Cakes) is a battercake made of flour and brown syrup deep-fried in oil. *Aluvas* (Coconut Halva) are thin, flat, diamond-shaped halvas, or wedges of rice flour, brown syrup and sugar cane. Coconut milk labouriously boiled down with jaggery and cashew nuts yields *kalu dodol* (Sweet Coconut Slices). *Kiribath* (Coconut Milk Rice Cakes), a festive dish of rice cooked in milk, is the first solid food fed to babies. A dish that originated in Malaya is *wattalappam*, an egg pudding rather like flan. *Kiri peni* or "curd and honey" is buffalo-milk yoghurt and brown syrup.

Sri Lankans are not the restaurant-goers one finds in other countries. The dishes in most restaurants aren't that much different than those at home, so dining out is more for business occasions rather than family get-togethers. Restaurants are very popular for "Chinese" foods though. These were contributed to the cuisine by early Chinese who came to open small shopfront businesses, married locally and taught their wives a few tricks. These days dishes like fried rice and chop suey are a tasty blend of both cultures. Thai

and French cuisines are finding their way to the island to satisfy the palates of visiting businessmen. A fusion cuisine is even being created at some of the large international hotels.

Festive foods have religious overtones in Sri Lanka. From the moment Buddhism was introduced into the island in the fourth century BC, the monks were considered worthy of the best sustenance people could offer. In the ancient monuments, one comes across large stone "rice canoes" that the devout filled with rice and other foods as gifts to the monks.

In a similar spirit, today, the monks are hosted to *dana* or ritual meals served in private homes. These include the housewife's best dishes, some prepared solely for monks. On the first birthday of a child, the monks are served an elaborate meal in their begging bowls. When a monk has finished, he holds his hand over his bowl. The finale comes when the father of the child ties a white thread around the little finger of the senior monk, and then around the little fingers of every other person in the room, ending with the child, uniting the entire room in a spiritual bond.

Ayurveda is a philosophy of healthy living that has found its way into Sri Lankan cooking. The word comes from *ayur*, meaning "life" and *veda*, which means "wisdom." The Ayurvedic philosophy is that

Five-star dining in Sri Lanka is centred around the larger hotels and resorts on the south and southwest coasts.

one's general well-being depends on one's choice of nourishment, lifestyle and habits. Keeping these in balance is the best way to minimise health problems.

Ayurvedic theory states that overall health is determined by the combination of five basic elements that are consumed from nature: air, fire, water, earth and ether. Everybody develops his or her own metabolic mix of elements by eating, drinking, breathing and so on. Imbalances from the optimal state result in the various manifestations of poor health. Therapy involves prescribing a diet combining ingredients that restore the balance of these basic elements. Ayurveda turns up in the selection of spices for various foods. The average curry may contain up to thirteen key ingredients: onions, garlic, chillies, lime, turmeric, cumin, fennel, coriander, fenugreek, ginger, pandanus (*rampe*), curry leaf (*karapincha*) and lemongrass (*sera*). Each of these has its own particular Ayurvedic effect as well as flavour.

Coursing through the cuisine of Sri Lanka is a great observance to details and tradition. It truly is like tasting history.

— Douglas Bullis

The Sri Lankan Kitchen

Despite a complex blend of spices, Sri Lankan dishes are simple to prepare

The traditional kitchen is at the back of, or separated from, the main house. Inside is a *lipa*, or open fire-place, with two or three trivets on which to place cooking pots. These trivets can be as simple as three stones, set tall enough to fuel a fire beneath, but just as often they are clay or metal tripods that do the same. Beneath the cooking area is a second shelf that holds the pots and fuel sticks to be used for that meal.

The fuel is usually the knotty stem of a fallen co-conut frond. The leaves are stripped off and the stem is cut into lengths of about one metre or smaller. The fire is usually started with *kolapu*, the fibrous and highly flammable but long-burning mesh from which the coconut's flower originally blossomed—although a handful of dry coconut leaves will do in a pinch.

Once the fire is going, one or two stems are pushed into, or withdrawn from, the trivet beneath the cooking pot, making a simple but quite sensitive temperature control. A coconut frond fire has the added virtue of imparting a delicate scent of its own to the dish bubbling away in the pot.

Most rural homes have an oven of some kind, usually a cube of brick or iron, with a door in front and a fire pit beneath. Temperatures are hard to con-trol, so the quality of breads and baked dishes can be rather uneven. Indeed, bread has never been a staple of the Sri Lankan diet, partly because of the rarity of wheat in this rice-dominated climate.

The traditional kitchen is quite a smoky affair, so it is usually ventilated with an open door or window and a clay vent pipe out the top. The fire area

ABOVE The *hiramanaya* or coconut scraper, is a short wooden bench with a metal extension and tooth.

LEFT An assortment of old pots and pans line the shelves of this period Dutch kitchen in the recently restored Historical Mansion in Galle on Sri Lanka's south coast.

doubles as the storage place for oft-used cooking accessories like a pot of salt brine just above the fire area with a ladle in it. Maldive fish and chillies hang on cords to keep them dry. **Stoppered jars** hold dry seeds and nuts like jack and cashew nut (*cadju*). Since years of cooking smoke

The *mirisgala* or grinding stone is still used today to grind spices in most kitchens.

have turned the entire interior almost black, it is an ill-lit place even on the sunniest day, and requires kerosene lamps in times of rain and at night.

Nearby is the *mirisgala*—literally, "**chilli stone**," though it is used for grinding many more items than chillies. The base is a heavy slab of granite or other very hard stone, about 30 cm (12 in) wide, and half as long again, and at least a palm's width thick. Onto this the cook places chillies and whole spices such as coriander, cumin, fennel, turmeric and whatever else must be mashed to a pulp. Applying to these a stone roller as hard as the grinding-stone itself, the cook sits on a very low stool called a *hiramanaya* and shifts her body forward and backward from the waist, rotating the roller a little with each pass, until the condiments are perfectly pulped.

Other ingredients like cowpea or green gram (mung beans) may also need pulverising but are too hard or large for the *mirisgala*. The cook then resorts to the *vangediya* or **mortar** and **pestle**. The mortar is a stone cylinder that reaches to her knees, whose mashing pit can be up to 30 cm (12 in) in diameter and the same distance deep. The *kitul*-wood pestle can be up to 1.5 metre (5 feet) in length and is usually bound with an iron ring at the pounding end to keep it from slivering. Her rhythmic boom-boom-boom as she pounds with the pestle can be heard all over the village—a sure signal to a husband and children that dinner is on the way.

Glistening black clay pots are everywhere in the traditional kitchen, usually stored upside-down on a platform outside. The rule of thumb is, the older the **clay pot**, the better the flavours. Some, like the *bath mutiya* or rice pot, have been shaped by centuries of experience guiding the potter's hand. It is a narrow-mouthed, chubby pot expressly made to heat rice until the water boils over. The erupting froth carries off chaff in the rice. The rotund shape ensures that the dripping froth doesn't fall on the fire. A similarly refined pot named the *nambiliya* has the express job of separating the rice from the stones. The cook swirls the grains round and round in the pot and slowly ladles off the rice at the top, until only the stones remain.

The kitchen has literally dozens of other pots and associated implements such as **mesh** or **coconut-husk ladles**, shallow dustpan-shaped *kulla* **baskets** used to throw rice up into the wind to rid it of chaff, and the *kalagediya* or **water pot** which one sees everywhere being carried by village girls on their way back home from the well. Although unbreakable aluminium has superseded the more fragile clay, the *kalagediya*'s shape is the same: an almost spherical container the size of a basketball with a very tiny neck to keep the water from spilling on the way home.

Although no end of kitchens such as this can be glimpsed during a simple walk around a village, their charm is not matched by their practicality. The smoke, the soot, the heat, the inconvenient postures—all these have defeated any attempts at improvement.

One improvement, though, has stuck: the **propane stove** that one sees everywhere in the "fancy goods" or household-wares shops that line the streets of every village and city. Most are two-burner outfits and quite economical compared with the enormous labour that accompanies traditional cooking methods. Propane stoves and kitchen counters are much better for the cook's health and posture, though they lack the built-in flavouring of the scent of a kitchen fire.

ABOVE A wooden pestle and mortar is used instead of the grinding stone for ingredients liable to release juices.

RIGHT To make *pittu* with a traditional *pittu bambuwa*, the flour and coconut mixture is stuffed into the bamboo which sits on a pot of boiling water. The steamed *pittu* are simply pushed out of the bamboo when cooked.

Cooking Methods

Although Sri Lankan cuisine uses a complex blend of spices and often requires several different cooking methods during the preparation of a single dish, it is much easier to prepare than some of the recipes would have you think. Most spices take a different amount of time to release their flavour and aroma. Hence it is important to follow the correct order given when adding spices to the cooking pan. To be sure of maximum flavour and aroma, it is best to buy whole spices and grind them just before cooking. Heat the spices in a dry pan until they begin to smell fragrant, shaking frequently and taking care that they do not burn. Cool and then grind them in a small electric grinder or blender.

The spices are usually then stir-fried or "tempered" in coconut oil, either alone or together with meat or vegetables. Most vegetable oil will substitute for coconut oil. Be sure to keep the temperature low and keep stirring the spices so they do not stick to the bottom of the pan. A wok is fine for stir-frying. If a wok is not available, a large thick-bottomed skillet or frying pan will do.

After tempering, most vegetable dishes and curries are left to simmer over low heat. Close the lids only part way, since an important quality to a Sri Lankan dish is the rich sauce, which can only come about by letting the steam escape. An exception to this is when using coconut milk, since coconut milk easily curdles or breaks down. It should be brought to a boil slowly, stirring frequently, lifting up a portion of the milk with a ladle and pouring it back into the pan. Once it has come to the boil, it should be simmered uncovered.

The seasonings can be adjusted just before the food is served. This may be as simple as a small sprinkle of the same spice used in the tempering or the addition of fried mustard seeds, dried chillies or curry leaves. The centrepiece (literally) of the Lankan dinner is a fluffy bowl of rice or *bath*. A rice cooker does almost as well the traditional *bath muttiya* pot.

Hoppers and *pittu* require specialised cooking pans. A very small wok can approximate a hopper pan, but it is best to try to find the real thing in Sri Lankan, or Indian, food stores. String hoppers can be approximated with a pasta maker using a vermicelli mould. Aluminium *pittu* steamers have largely replaced the traditional *pittu bambuwa*, as they are able to make five rolls of *pittu* at a time.

— **Douglas Bullis**

Sri Lankan Ingredients

A guide to the essential ingredients used in Sri Lankan cooking

Asian eggplants are the long or slender, purple-skinned variety. Round Mediterranean eggplants may be used instead but these have more moisture than the Asian variety. They should be lightly salted and allowed to "sweat" for about 30 minutes to remove some of the moisture before cooking.

Banana blossoms, the unopened flowers of the banana plant, taste like artichokes and are a popular salad ingredient in Asia. To prepare them, remove the outer petals of the bud, quarter the tender heart and slice it lengthwise. If not using immediately, soak the slices in cold water or sprinkle lime juice over them to prevent discolouration. Crisp cabbage leaves make a reasonable substitute.

Belimbi is a pale green, acidic fruit about 5–7 cm (2–3 in) long, often added to curries, soups and pickles. It belongs to the same family as the starfruit and is sometimes called baby starfruit. Belimbi is used as a souring agent and also has thickening properties. Tamarind pulp may be substituted.

Cardamom pod is an aromatic spice pod native to India. The more common cardamom pods are small, green or straw-coloured, and contain a dozen or so tiny, intensely aromatic black seeds. Cardamon pods are used to flavour curries and desserts—giving foods a heady, sweet aroma. Whole pods are bruised lightly with a cleaver or a pestle before use. Do not buy ground cardamom as it is virtually flavourless compared with the heavenly fragrance of the freshly roasted and ground whole spice. Cardamom pods are available in health food stores and Indian grocers.

Cashew nuts are used to provide substance as well as a nutty fragrance to curry gravies. Recipes that call for cashew nuts require fresh, unsalted and unroasted cashew nuts.

Celery grows in bunches of long, ribbed stalks with leafy tops and ranges in colour from white to green—the darker its colour, the stonger its flavour. One of the most popular vegetables in the Western world, celery has an herbal, astringent flavour and succulent, crisp texture. It is usually eaten raw, but it's also delicious cooked in soups. Celery should be firm and tightly formed, with evenly shaped stalks and fresh-looking leaves. The tougher outer stalks are the best to cook with—just pull them off at the base and use a peeler to remove any tough strings. The inner, more tender stalks are for eating raw. Trim the ends and wash to rid of grit and dirt. The leafy tops can be used in salads.

Dried chillies

Fresh finger-length chillies

Bird's-eye chillies

Chillies are used both fresh and dried in Sri Lankan cooking. The commonly-used fresh green and red finger-length chillies are moderately hot. Green chillies are used in vegetable curries, and when finely sliced, in *sambols* and tomato and onion salads. Red chillies are dried and either coarsely crushed for meat dishes, or ground for fish and meat curries. Tiny red, green or yellow-orange bird's-eye chillies are very hot, designed for strong palates. Dried chillies are usually cut into lengths and soaked in warm water to soften before use. They have a very different flavour from fresh chilies. If the chillies called for in a recipe are simply too hot for one's palate, either reduce the quantity or slice them in half lengthwise and discard the seeds. **Chilli powder** is a hot seasoning made from ground dried red chillies. **Chilli flakes** are made from dried chillies that have been crushed leaving whole seeds and pieces of dried chilli flesh.

Chilli flakes

Chilli powder

Cinnamon is lighter in colour, thinner, and more expensive than cassia bark, which is often sold as cinnamon. Cassia bark has a stronger flavour than cinnamon, but makes an acceptable substitute. Do not use ground cinnamon as a substitute where cinnamon sticks are called for.

Cloves are actually dried flower buds of an aromatic bush. This small, brown, nail-shaped spice emits a floral, spicy fragrance and is used in spice blends. They are often added whole to curries for flavouring (they are not eaten if used whole). Freshly ground clove is a common ingredient in curries, while whole cloves are used while simmering curries, making savoury rice and in "devilled" or spicy-hot minced meats. Pre-ground clove loses much of the original flavour.

Coriander seeds are round and beige and are an essential ingredient in many Sri Lankan meat and fish curries. When ground they release a warm, nutty, slightly citrus-like aroma. Whole coriander seeds have a stronger flavour than ground coriander powder, although the latter may also be used.

Coconut milk or **coconut cream** is available fresh or canned and in packets which are quick, convenient and quite tasty. Canned or packet coconut cream and milk comes in various consistencies, depending on the brand and you will need to try them out and adjust the thickness by adding water as needed. In general, add 1 cup of water to 1 cup of canned or packet **coconut cream** to obtain **thick coconut milk**, and 2 cups of water to 1 cup of coconut cream to obtain thin coconut milk. Freshly **grated coconut** is obtained by grating fresh coconut flesh. Freshly grated coconut can be purchased in many Asian markets. **Desiccated coconut** is grated coconut flesh that has been finely ground and dried. Sweetened and unsweetened coconut flakes of several sizes are sold in packets, usually in the baking section of supermarkets.

Cumin seeds are pale brown to black in colour and ridged on the outside. They impart an earthy flavour and are used whole, or roasted and ground to a fine powder. Cumin seeds are usually partnered with coriander seeds in basic spice mixes, and are often dry-roasted or fried in oil to intensify their flavour.

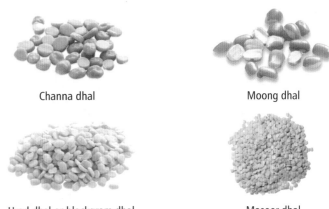

Channa dhal

Moong dhal

Urad dhal or blackgram dhal

Masoor dhal

Dhal, sometimes spelled dal, is a term that covers a variety of dried lentils. The major ones are: **Channa dhal** (Bengal gram), which resembles a small yellow pea and is often sold split and used as a seasoning. If unavailable, substitute yellow split peas. **Moong dhal** (green gram or mung bean) is the small green mung bean that is sprouted to make bean sprouts. **Urad dhal** (black gram) is sold either with its black skin still on (substitute with black lentils) or when husked, is creamy white in colour (substitute with white lentils). **Masoor dhal** (also known as mysore dhal) is salmon-pink in colour, cook quickly and they turn golden and mushy when cooked. Substitute red or green lentils. The various types of dhal can usually be found in Indian specialty stores, supermarkets and health food stores.

Curry leaves are an important herb in Sri Lankan cooking. The taste is a cross between basil and mint. The fresh small, dark green leaf has a distinctive flavour which is sadly missing from the dried form. When a sprig of curry leaves is called for in a recipe, this means 8–12 individual leaves.

sizes and the very small ones have the heads and tails attached. Look for dried prawns that are pink and plump. Better quality dried prawns are bright orange in colour and shelled.

Dried prawns are tiny, orange-coloured sun-dried saltwater prawns. They keep for several months and should be soaked in water for 5 minutes to soften slightly before use. Dried prawns come in various

Fennel is similar in appearance to cumin although slightly longer and fatter. Fennel has a sweet fragrance that is similar to aniseed. The seeds are used whole or ground.

Fenugreek seeds are flat and slightly rectangular, about 3 mm (⅛ in) across, light brown in colour, with a deep furrow along their lengths. They are used in Indian cuisines and are quite bitter, so use sparingly.

Garlic is minced or mashed when used in Sri Lankan cuisine. It is stir-fried with other ingredients, to which are then added curries and the meat, fish or vegetable ingredients. Asian garlics are somewhat smaller than Western, so a dish that calls for 3 cloves of garlic will do with two if cooked in Europe or North America.

Ghee is clarified butter with the milk solids removed. Widely used in Indian and Sri Lankan cooking, it can be heated to high temperatures without burning and adds a rich and delicious flavour to food. While ghee can be found in many Asian food stores, it may be substituted with butter or vegetable oil.

Ginger is usually sliced thinly, minced or crushed with garlic before stir-frying. Fresh ginger root is a flavour enhancer for meat and fish curries. The skin should be peeled before slicing or mincing. Dried ginger is used more for sweets than for curries.

Jaggery is made from crystallised *kitul* palm sap. Palm sugar—made from palmyra palm sap—can be substituted. If none of these are available, use soft brown sugar or maple sugar even though the flavour will lack the complex nuances of the *kitul* sap.

Jackfruit is a large, green fruit with a tough, knobbly skin, which reveals a yellow, segmented flesh when opened. It has a taste that is naturally sweet. Recipes that call for young jack require that the fruit be scraped away from the tough skin and chopped or minced, seeds included.

The fully ripe mature jack consists of two cooking elements, the pericarps or drupes, which are the sweet fleshy fruit, and the tender nut-flavoured seeds. Both are used in recipes, but should be washed before further preparation. Readily available fresh in South-East Asia, the fruit can be purchased canned in the West.

Ragi flour is known as finger millet in English. It is a grain with a flavour and colour similar to rye which is used in the preparation of some unleavened breads. Substitute with unbleached whole wheat flour.

Lemongrass is a fragrant, lemony stalk that is either bruised and used whole in soups or curries, or sliced and ground as part of a basic spice mix. It is usually sold in bunches of 3–4 stems in the supermarket. The tough outer layers should be peeled away and only the thick lower third of the stem used. Always slice the stems before grinding to get a smooth paste. Lemongrass is becoming more widely available in specialty and Asian foodstores and is worth looking for. Powdered lemongrass does not have quite the same aromatic flavour.

Limes of various types are used in cooking, but Sri Lankan recipes call for the thin-skinned, light green calamansi limes whose fruit is about the size of a walnut and have a less acidic, more fragrant juice.

Maldive fish is bonito tuna dried in the roaring hot sun of the Maldives—it dries so hard it needs no salt. It is usually finely grated or ground in Sri Lankan recipes. If Maldive fish is unavailable, freeze-dried fish flakes or dried prawns can substitute.

Mustard oil is vegetable oil infused with ground mustard seeds and used for cooking as well as preserving. The flavour is distinct and is worth looking for in Indian specialty stores; if mustard oil is not available, substitute any refined vegetable oil.

Mustard seeds are either brownish-black (above right) or yellow (above left). Sri Lankan cooks use both types. Sometimes they are popped in hot oil before garlic and onions are added for tempering. Other times they are ground and added to a curry powder. They are also used whole in making pickles and cabbage dishes. Try to use the type specified.

Okra is also known as ladies' fingers and is a variety of banana. It is a green, curved, ridged vegetable, ranging from 6 to 20 cm (2½ to 8 inches) in length. It acquires a slimy texture when cooked. This can be minimised by soaking them for five minutes in a bath made of the juice of one lemon in 4 cups (1 litre) of water. Pat dry and cook as normal. Okra has long been popular in Sri Lanka and South-East Asia as a vegetable.

Pandanus leaves impart a subtle fragrance and a green hue to dishes.

They are also used to add flavour to boiled rice. They are usually tied in a knot and then added to a liquid recipe. Remove the leaves before serving. Fresh and frozen pandanus leaves are becoming more widely available in specialty and Asian food-stores. Bottled pandanus extract can be substituted in desserts, but if fresh or dried pandanus leaves are not available, omit them from savoury dishes. Vanilla essence may be substituted in dessert recipes.

Palm sugar is sold as a solid block or cylinder of sugar made from the sap of the coconut or arenga sugar palm. It varies in colour from gold to light brown and has a faint caramel taste. To measure, hard palm sugar should be shaved, grated or melted in a microwave oven. Substitute dark brown sugar.

Pumpkin is a member of the gourd, squash and melon family. Possessing a sweet flavour similar to that of butternut squash, this firm-textured vegetable is used in soups, stews and sweetened puddings. Though hardly the same, the best substitutes are butternut and acorn squash.

Sea salt Sri Lankan rural cooks do not use crystal salt, they keep a clay pot of brine directly above the cooking area, from which they ladle out as much as they want.

Tamarind pulp is the fruit pulp found inside the tamarind tree seed pod. It is sold dried in packets or jars and generally still has some seeds and pod fibres mixed in with the dried pulp. It is used as a souring agent in many dishes. The pods are often chewed and sucked like hard candy by people working in the hot sun to keep their mouths from going dry. To obtain **tamarind juice**, mash the pulp in warm water, strain and discard the seeds or fibres. If using already cleaned tamarind pulp, slightly reduce the amounts called for in the recipes. Dried tamarind pulp keeps indefinitely in an airtight container. Tamarind pulp is readily available in specialty and Asian foodstores.

Turmeric is a root similar to ginger but with a bright yellow to orange colour and a strong woody flavour. Turmeric has antiseptic and astringent qualities, and stains permanently, so scrub your knife blade, hands and chopping board immediately after handling. Purchase fresh turmeric root as needed as the flavour fades after a few days. Substitute 1 teaspoon turmeric powder for 2.5 cm (1 in) of the fresh root.

Vinegar is used to make condiments or as a preservative. Rice vinegar, with its mild and faintly fragrance, is the preferred vinegar for Sri Lankan recipes. If unavailable, substitute Balsamic vinegar or distilled white vinegar. **White vinegar** is made from glutinous rice and has a mild, sweet flavour. It is colourless and is one of the definitive ingredients used in sweet and sour sauce. Substitute with Japanese rice vinegar or white wine vinegar.

Basic Recipes

Roasted Curry Powder

This is used as an ingredient in curries or can be sprinkled on vegetables before serving.

½ teaspoon fennel seeds
½ teaspoon cumin seeds
½ teaspoon fenugreek seeds
1½ teaspoons cinnamon powder
6 cardamom pods
100 g (½ cup) coriander seeds
6 cloves

Dry-roast all the ingredients in a frying pan over low heat, stirring constantly, until the spices become a deep golden colour. Grind them to a fine powder in a mortar or blender. Store in an air-tight container.

Unroasted Curry Powder

100 g (½ cup) coriander seeds
½ teaspoon fennel seeds
½ teaspoon cumin seeds
½ teaspoon fenugreek seeds
½ teaspoon cashew nuts
1 medium cinnamon stick
1 stalk lemongrass, tender inner part of bottom third only
6 cardamom pods
6 cloves
½ teaspoon fresh ginger
1½ tablespoons peppercorns
½ teaspoon mustard seeds
80 g (½ cup) ground uncooked rice

Place all the ingredients except the ground rice in a blender and blend to a fine powder. Stir in the ground rice. Store in an air-tight container. If kept frozen, this curry blend will remain fresh for a long period of time.

Two or three sambols or dips, are served with every Sri Lankan meal.

Bitter Gourd Sambol

250 g (8 oz) bitter gourd, finely sliced
1 teaspoon turmeric powder
Oil, for frying
150 g (¾ cup) finely sliced onion
2 green finger-length chillies, finely sliced
1 teaspoon Maldive fish, or dried prawns/fish,
   ground to a powder in a blender (optional)
1 teaspoon lime juice
1 teaspoon salt

Rub the bitter gourd slices with the turmeric powder
and fry them until golden brown and crisp. Mix the
onion, chillies, Maldive fish or dried prawns, lime juice
and salt together in a separate bowl. Add the fried
gourd and mix well. Store in a sealed container in a
cool place until needed.

Dried Chilli Sambol

200 g (1 cup) dried red finger-length chillies
Pinch of salt
200 g (1 cup) finely chopped onion
3 tablespoons Maldive fish, or dried prawns/fish,
   ground to a powder in a blender
1 teaspoon lemon juice

Coarsely grind the dried red chillies with the salt.
Add all the other ingredients. Stir until well mixed.
Store in a covered container in a cool place and use as
desired.

Bird's-eye Chilli Sambol

100 g (½ cup) bird's-eye chillies
½ onion, sliced
1 teaspoon pepper
3 tablespoons lime juice
Salt, to taste

Grind the chillies and onion in a mortar or blender
until fine. Add the pepper, lime juice and salt. Best
when served freshly made. Store in a covered
container in a cool place and use as desired.

Fresh Coconut Sambol

1 teaspoon chopped dried red finger-length chilli
1 tablespoon finely chopped onion
1 teaspoon pepper
1 teaspoon dried Maldive Fish or dried prawns/fish,
   ground to a powder in a blender
200 g (2 cups) freshly grated coconut or 125 g (¾ cup)
   unsweetened desiccated coconut, moistened
3 tablespoons lime juice
Salt, to taste

Grind the chilli, onion, pepper and Maldive fish or dried
prawns in a mortar or blender until smooth, adding a
little oil if necessary to keep the blades turning. Add
the coconut and season with the lime juice and salt.
Mix well by hand to ensure the coconut is well coated.
Best served freshly made.

Wing Bean Sambol

500 g (2½ cups) finely sliced wing beans
    or green beans
Salted water for soaking wing beans
150 g (1½ cups) freshly grated coconut
3 tablespoons Maldive fish, or dried prawns/fish,
    ground to a powder in a blender
100 g (½ cup) sliced onion
1 teaspoon crushed pepper
1 green finger-length chilli, sliced
1 teaspoon lemon juice
Salt, to taste

Soak the wing beans in the salted water for several
minutes. Drain and squeeze out the excess water. Mix
all the ingredients together and adjust the seasoning.
Store in a sealed container in a cool place until needed.

Roasted Coconut Sambol

200 g (2 cups) freshly grated coconut, dry-roasted
3 bird's-eye chillies, chopped
1 teaspoon Maldive fish, or dried prawns/fish
1 teaspoon pepper
2 cloves garlic, chopped
1 sprig curry leaves
3 tablespoons lime juice
Salt, to taste

Blend all the ingredients in a blender until smooth (add
more lime juice if more liquid is needed). Store in a
covered container in a cool place and use as desired.

Onion and Maldive Fish Sambol

3 tablespoons oil
1 kg (5 cups) finely chopped onion
Salt, to taste
8 cardamom pods, smashed in a mortar
1 medium cinnamon stick
4 cloves
1 sprig curry leaves
5 cm (2 in) pandanus leaf
100 g (⅓ cup) Maldive fish or dried prawns/fish,
    ground to a powder in a blender
2 tablespoons chilli powder
4 tablespoons tamarind juice (page 27)
50 g (¼ cup) sugar

Heat the oil in a frying pan until hot and stir-fry the
onion, salt, cardamom, cinnamon, cloves, curry leaves
and pandanus leaf until golden brown. Drain the
excess oil, leaving about 1 teaspoon in the pan. Stir
in the Maldive fish or dried prawns, chilli powder and
tamarind juice, and stir-fry over high heat for 4 to 6
minutes until the mixture turns dark brown and the
liquid evaporates. Stir in the sugar and immediately
remove from the heat. Allow to cool before storing in
sterilised storage jars.

Coconut Milk Gravy

1 tablespoon fenugreek seeds
2 cups (500 ml) chicken stock
1 large onion, finely chopped
2 sprigs curry leaves
2 pieces pandanus leaf
3 cloves garlic, finely chopped
1 short cinnamon stick
4 cardamom pods, smashed in a mortar
2 green finger-length chillies, deseeded
    and finely sliced
1 teaspoon turmeric powder
2 teaspoons Maldive fish, or dried prawns/fish,
    ground to a powder in a blender
2 cups (500 ml) coconut milk
Salt and lemon juice, to taste

Wash the fenugreek seeds and soak them in the
chicken stock in a saucepan for 30 minutes. Add all
the remaining ingredients except the coconut milk,
salt and lemon juice. Bring to a boil and simmer on
very low heat until the onions are tender.

Add the coconut milk and return to a boil, then
reduce the heat and simmer for about 5 minutes.
Remove from the heat and allow to cool slightly.
Add the lemon juice and salt to taste.

Melon Ginger Sauce

1 teaspoon fresh ginger, chopped	200 g (1 cup) diced fresh melon
1 cup (250 ml) water	1 teaspoon lemon juice
2 tablespoons cornflour	Salt and pepper, to taste

Banana Blossom Sambol

2 fresh banana blossoms (about 500 g/8 oz)
Lemon water, made with juice of 1 lemon and
    4 cups (1 litre) water
Oil, for deep-frying
200 g (1 cup) finely chopped onion
3 green finger-length chillies, finely sliced
6 tablespoons lime juice
Salt and pepper, to taste

Remove the outer red petals of the banana blossoms,
quarter the tender heart and halve it lengthwise.
Wash in the lemon water. Drain, pat dry and then cut
crosswise into coarse slices. Deep-fry the slices until
golden brown. Remove and set aside. Mix the onion,
chillies, lime juice, salt and pepper together. Add to the
fried banana blossoms and mix well. Store in a covered
container in a cool place and use as desired.

Saffron Lemongrass Sauce

1 cup (250 ml) chicken stock
½ stalk lemongrass, tender inner part of bottom
    third only
5 saffron threads
1 tablespoon cornflour
1½ tablespoons lime juice

Boil the chicken stock in a small pan with the lemongrass and saffron, about 15 to 20 minutes. Dissolve
the cornflour in a little water, add to the stock and
simmer for 2 to 3 minutes until it thickens. Remove
from the heat, add the lime juice, strain, and serve as
an accompaniment to other dishes.

Bring the ginger and water to a boil. Dissolve the
cornflour in a small amount of water and add to the
boiling liquid. Stir with a whisk while simmering for 5
minutes. Remove from the heat. Add the diced melon
and lemon juice. Season with salt and pepper and
serve as an accompaniment to other dishes.

Young Jackfruit Pickles

500 g (1 lb) tender young jackfruit
Salt, to taste
3 tablespoons vinegar
200 g (1 cup) chopped onion
50 g (⅔ cup) chopped green finger-length chillies
50 g (¼ cup) sugar
2 tablespoons mustard seeds
3½ tablespoons chopped fresh ginger
1 teaspoon peppercorns, ground
½ teaspoon chopped garlic

Boil the jackfruit in a little water, with the salt and vinegar, until it is just tender. Drain and reserve the water. Discard the outer skin of the jackfruit and slice thinly. Blanch the onion and chilli in the reserved water. Remove the onion and chilli and mix with the rest of the ingredients. Add the jackfruit and some of the reserved water. Store in a sealed container in a cool place until needed. Serve as an accompaniment to main dishes.

Pickled Eggplant

2 tablespoons oil
2 large Asian eggplants (about 500 g/1 lb total),
    thinly sliced
1 small onion, sliced into thin rings
1 teaspoon mustard seeds, finely ground
1 teaspoon sugar
½ teaspoon turmeric powder
3 tablespoons vinegar
2–3 green finger-length chillies, halved lengthwise
2 tablespoons dried prawns or Maldive fish, ground
    to a powder in a blender
Salt and pepper, to taste

Heat the oil and fry the eggplant until golden brown. Remove and set aside to cool.

In the same pan, add the onion and stir-fry until soft. Add the remaining ingredients and the fried eggplant. Cook for 10 to 15 minutes. Serve at room temperature as an accompaniment to other dishes.

Rice & Bread Recipes

Butter Rice

2½ tablespoons butter or ghee
½ onion, finely chopped
2 sprigs curry leaves
2 cardamom pods, smashed in a mortar
2 cloves
½ small cinnamon stick
500 g (2½ cups) uncooked Basmati or
    other long-grained rice, washed
3 cups (750 ml) chicken stock
1 teaspoon salt, or to taste
1 small potato, peeled and sliced into
    matchsticks, then deep-fried
1 tablespoon dry-roasted unsalted
    cashew nuts
½ teaspoon sultana raisins

Heat the butter and fry half the onion until golden. Add the curry leaves, cardamom, cloves, cinnamon and rice. Fry over medium heat for 5 minutes, stirring continuously, then add the chicken stock and salt. Bring to a boil, reduce the heat, cover and simmer for 30 minutes.

Meanwhile, in a separate frying pan, fry the remaining onion and set aside to be used as garnish.

When the rice is cooked, remove the spices, place the rice on a platter and garnish with the fried potato matchsticks, dry-roasted cashew nuts, sultana raisins and reserved fried onion.

Coconut Milk Rice Cakes

Hiding behind its simplicity of preparation, *kiri bath* is both a dietary staple and a food with ceremonial and spiritual significance which, according to historical evidence, has been a part of Sri Lankan culinary tradition for the last 2,500 years. Even today, it is the first food to be eaten on Sinhalese New Year when it is consumed with specially prescribed accompaniments, and it is also commonly eaten for breakfast on the first day of each month.

1 kg (5 cups) uncooked glutinous rice
6 cups (1.5 litres) thin coconut milk
½ teaspoon salt
1 cup (250 ml) thick coconut milk
2 teaspoons oil

Coconut Milk Rice Cakes accompanied by Dried Chilli Sambol (bottom left) and Tamarind Claypot Fish (bottom right)

Soak the rice in water for 30 minutes, then drain. Place the rice in a pan, add the thin coconut milk and simmer on low heat for 30 minutes. Mix the salt and thick coconut milk and add to the boiling rice. Reduce the heat and cook until the rice is well done, about 10 minutes.

Smear a little oil on a banana leaf or a waxed paper, pour the rice on it, flatten the rice with a spatula to about 2 cm (¾ in) thick. Let cool, cut into diamond shapes and serve with Fresh Coconut Sambol.

Ragi Flour Flatbreads

Ragi is one of the staple food grains in Sri Lanka, especially in the drier areas, and is higher in protein, fat and minerals than rice or corn. It is often available from Indian and Sri Lankan foodstores. Makes 4 servings.

250 g (2 cups) ragi flour or whole wheat flour
250 g (2 cups) rice flour
50 g (½ cup) freshly grated or unsweetened desiccated coconut
1 teaspoon salt
Water as needed
Ghee or oil as needed

Sift both varieties of flour into a bowl and mix with the grated coconut and salt. Add sufficient quantities of water and ghee to form a stiff dough that does not stick to the hands. Knead well.

Shape into even-sized balls and flatten them into circular shapes 6 to 12 mm (¼ to ½ in) thick and 8 to 10 cm (3 to 4 in) in diameter. Sear both sides on a hot griddle or cast-iron frying pan, about 2 to 3 minutes each side. Finish by placing both sides briefly above a naked flame.

Seasoned Coconut and Rice Flour Flatbreads

It seems every bread maker has his own special way of turning and slapping a as it cooks. Breads should be eaten hot. This recipe makes about 5 flatbreads.

400 g (3 cups) dry-roasted rice flour
180 g (1¾ cups) freshly grated coconut
¾ teaspoon salt
⅔ cup (150 ml) water
1 green finger-length chilli, chopped
40 g (¼ cup) thinly sliced onion
2 teaspoons dried prawns
5 curry leaves, finely sliced into threads

Mix the flour and grated coconut together in a bowl. Add the salt and enough water to make a stiff dough. Stir-fry the chilli, onion, dried prawns and curry leaves for several minutes until the onion is translucent. Mix these into the dough and knead well.

Shape into 10 even-sized balls and flatten on a waxed paper into circular shapes 6 to 12 mm (¼ to ½ in) thick and 8 to 10 cm (3 to 4 in) in diameter. Sear on a hot griddle or cast-iron frying pan for 3 to 4 minutes then flip and cook the other side. Finish by placing both sides briefly above a naked flame. Serve with a meat or fish curry.

Crispy Dosai Pancakes

This fermented bread originated in northern Sri Lanka but has now migrated to almost every corner of the country. Normally dosais are served with a few hot sambols on a stainless steel plate, or on a banana leaf. If desired, they can be stuffed with a richly spiced potato and Dhal Stew or a boneless chicken curry.

Mix the husked black gram (which will now be white) and the rice. Soak in a large amount of water for at least 2 hours. Drain and grind the soaked ingredients in a blender with enough water to form a batter of pancake consistency. Blend in the flour and baking powder (if using) and leave to ferment in a large bowl for at least 3 hours (preferably overnight).

Heat the oil and fry the onion, chillies, curry leaves, cumin seeds and mustard seeds. Add these to the fermented batter. Mix in the turmeric and salt, adding water if necessary to retain a pancake-batter consistency.

Heat a hot plate or griddle pan (or non-stick frying pan) to high heat and smear a little oil on the surface. When the oil smokes, reduce the heat slightly. Pour a ladleful of batter onto the hot plate, spreading it quickly, using a spiral motion, outwards until it measures about 15 cm (6 in) in diameter. Pour a few drops of oil on and around the edges of the dosai and cook it until lightly golden. Fold the dosai in half or roll it into a tube. Serve hot with sambol accompaniments.

100 g (½ cup) husked black gram (*urad dhal*) lentils
100 g (½ cup) uncooked rice
100 g (⅔ cup) wheat flour
Pinch of baking powder (optional)
2 tablespoons oil
50 g (¼ cup) chopped onion

2–3 dried red finger-length chillies, broken in two
1 sprig curry leaves
½ teaspoon cumin seeds
½ teaspoon mustard seeds
1 teaspoon turmeric powder
1½ teaspoons salt, or to taste
Oil, for frying

Rice Flour Hoppers

Hoppers—a favourite breakfast dish in Sri Lanka—are small bowl-shaped rice flour pancakes which are eaten with curries and sambols (it is usual to serve each person one hopper with an egg baked in its centre and the rest plain). Although the traditional method of preparing them requires placing a hopper pan on hot coals (with more coals on its lid), hoppers may be prepared on regular stoves. Hopper pans are readily available from Indian and Sri Lankan foodstores.

500 g (4 cups) rice flour
¼ cup (60 ml) palm toddy or 1 teaspoon
    dried yeast
2 teaspoons sugar
¾ cup (200 ml) thin coconut milk
Salt, to taste
2 cups (500 ml) thick coconut milk

Combine the rice flour, toddy or yeast, sugar and thin coconut milk in a mixing bowl. Stir to form a thick batter. Cover with a damp tea towel and leave to stand overnight, or 6 to 8 hours, by which time the batter should have doubled in volume. When the batter has risen, soften it by working in the salt and thick coconut milk to form a thinner batter.

Heat a greased hopper pan (or any high-sided, small hemispherical pan with two handles) over low heat. Pour a large spoonful of batter into the pan and, being mindful to use oven gloves or pot holders, pick up the pan by both handles and swirl the pan so the batter rides up the sides almost to the rim. Replace the pan over the heat, cover with any saucepan lid, and cook until the surface of the hopper at the bottom is almost firm and the sides are crispy and brown, about 5 minutes.

Remove the hopper with a metal spatula (a curved instrument would be ideal) and serve hot. Grease the pan again and repeat with the remaining batter. Makes about 20 hoppers.

String Hoppers

500 g (4 cups) rice flour
1½ teaspoons salt, or to taste
200 ml (¾ cup) boiling water, or as
    needed

Warm the flour in a low oven, then sift into a bowl. Add the salt, then slowly add the hot water and work into a soft dough. Place the dough in a string hopper or vermicelli press and press the plunger to squeeze small, flat noodle patties onto hopper mats.

Place the mats in a steamer, or a large pot with a trivet at the bottom and sufficient water to just reach the trivet's rungs. Steam until the strings are fully cooked and springy in texture, about 10 minutes.

Remove the string hoppers from the steamer and serve hot with Fresh Coconut Sambol (recipe on page 30) and Coconut Milk Gravy (recipe on page 32).

An Egg Hopper (above), accompanied by Coconut Milk Gravy (upper of two side dips, see recipe page 32) and Onion and Maldive Fish Sambol (lower of two side dips, see recipe page 31), and String Hoppers (below right).

Soups

Tomato Soup with Fennel

2 tablespoons butter
100 g (½ cup) chopped onion
100 g (1 cup) diced carrot
½ teaspoon minced garlic
½ teaspoon chopped celery
2 tablespoons flour
2 large tomatoes, coarsely chopped
2 tablespoons dry-roasted fennel
    powder
6 cups (1.5 litres) chicken stock
Salt and pepper, to taste

Melt the butter in a thick-bottomed pan. Add the onion, carrot, garlic and celery, and brown lightly. Mix in the flour with a wooden spoon. Cook to a blond-brown colour. Add the tomatoes and fennel powder, cover with a lid and cook for 8 minutes on low heat.

Remove the lid and add the chicken stock. Stir well and bring to a boil. Simmer for 15 minutes and skim the foam and oils from the surface. Remove from the heat and pass through a fine strainer. Return the strained stock to the pan and bring to a boil. Season with salt and pepper to taste. Serve hot.

Pumpkin Soup with Prawns (left) and Tomato Soup with Fennel (right).

Pumpkin Soup with Prawns

A spicy rendition of a basic vegetable and prawn soup that goes well with any bread of your choice.

4 tablespoons butter
2 small onions, coarsely chopped
100 g (1½ cups) leeks, coarsely chopped
100 g (2 cups) celery, coarsely chopped
10 cloves garlic
2 tablespoons flour
250 g (2 cups) cubed pumpkin
4 teaspoons dry-roasted coriander powder
4 teaspoons dry-roasted cumin powder
3 teaspoons dry-roasted chilli powder
6 cups (1.5 litres) chicken stock
Salt and pepper, to taste
½ teaspoon chopped garlic
15 fresh prawns, peeled and deveined
4 teaspoons sesame seeds, dry-roasted
3 tablespoons dry-roasted unsweetened
    desiccated coconut

Melt 3 tablespoons of the butter in a thick-bottomed pan. Add the onions, leeks, celery and garlic, and cook slowly over low heat until the juices are released. Stir in the flour and mix until the mixture thickens slightly. Cook for several more minutes until the mixture turns pale brown in colour. Add the pumpkin, then the coriander, cumin and chilli powders. Cover with a lid and simmer on low heat for 8 to 10 minutes. Remove the lid and add the chicken stock. Stir well and bring to a boil. Add the salt and pepper. Simmer for 15 minutes, skimming the foam and oil that forms on the surface. Remove from the heat, transfer to a blender and blend until smooth.

To prepare the prawns, heat the remaining 1 tablespoon of butter in a pan and stir-fry the garlic. Add the prawns and stir-fry briefly until the prawns change colour, about 3 minutes. Divide the prawns and garlic evenly into the soup bowls and pour the pumpkin soup on top. Garnish with the dry-roasted sesame seeds and desiccated coconut. Serve hot.

Rich Seafood Soup

Jaffna, in the north of Sri Lanka, is famous for its *kool*, or rich seafood soup. Originating from the Tamil fishing communities of the north, this soup is traditionally made with whatever leftover seafood is available, from crabs and prawns to fish meat and fish heads.

6 cups (1.5 litres) fish or prawn stock, or water
3 heaping tablespoons uncooked red (or other) rice
100 g (1 cup) green beans, sliced
50 g (1 cup) cubed potato
100 g (1 cup) cubed young jackfruit flesh
1 teaspoon turmeric powder
½ teaspoon potato flour or tapioca flour
Salt, to taste
3–4 dried red finger-length chillies, broken into pieces
1 tablespoon tamarind juice (page 27)
500 g (1 lb) grouper, cod or other mild-flavoured fish, cubed
200 g (7 oz) fresh prawns, peeled and deveined

In a large pan, bring the fish stock, rice, green beans, potato and jackfruit flesh to a boil. Reduce the heat and simmer for another 5 minutes.

Add the turmeric powder, flour, salt, chillies and tamarind juice, and simmer for a further 2 minutes. Add the fish, simmer for 10 minutes then add the prawns and cook until the prawns are cooked, about 5 minutes. Serve hot.

Curry Leaf Congee

200 g (1 cup) uncooked long-grained rice
3 cups (750 ml) water
40 g (1 cup) fresh curry leaves
3 cups (750 ml) water
1¾ cups (400 ml) fresh milk
3 cloves
1 teaspoon salt, or to taste
1 tablespoon jaggery (substitute shaved
    palm sugar or dark brown sugar)

Wash and drain the rice, then boil it in 3 cups (750 ml) water until the grains are quite soft.

Wash and then purée the curry leaves in a blender with 3 cups (750 ml) water and pass the mixture through a fine strainer into the cooked rice. Add the milk, cloves and salt, and mix well. Bring to a boil and simmer for 3 minutes. Remove from the heat and serve with jaggery or shaved palm sugar.

Coconut Milk Congee

Pol kiri kanda is often taken for breakfast, especially during the hot season as it is considered a cooling food.

200 g (1 cup) uncooked long-grained rice
6 cups (1.5 litres) water
2.5 cm (1 in) fresh ginger, finely sliced
½ onion, thinly sliced and fried in a little oil until crispy
3 cloves garlic, whole
Pinch of salt
1¾ cups (400 ml) thick coconut milk
1 tablespoon jaggery (shaved palm sugar or
    dark brown sugar may be substituted)

Wash and drain the rice, then boil it in 3 cups (750 ml) water until the grains are quite soft.

Strain the rice and purée it with 1½ cups (375 ml) of the water. Add the ginger, crispy fried onion, garlic, salt an coconut milk to the remaining water, and bring to a boil. Add the rice purée and simmer for 3 minutes. Remove from the heat and serve with jaggery or shaved palm sugar.

Curry Leaf Congee   Coconut Milk Congee

Seafood Dishes

Spicy Fish Stew

Seer or Spanish mackerel is arguably Sri Lanka's tastiest fish. Certainly it is one of the most popular with visitors, many of whom are accustomed to seeing it served pan-fried. There are, however, many other ways to bring out its delicious flavours, such as in this delicate stew recipe.

700 g (1½ lbs) fresh Spanish mackerel,
    kingfish or cod fillets
Salt, to taste
1 teaspoon ground white pepper
3 tablespoons oil
2 large onions, 1 diced and 1 sliced into rings
2 sprigs curry leaves
4 cloves garlic, minced
2 green finger-length chillies, finely sliced
4 cardamom pods, smashed in a mortar
½ teaspoon fenugreek seeds
1 stalk lemongrass, tender inner part of
    bottom third only, finely sliced
2 teaspoons coriander powder
1 teaspoon cumin powder
½ teaspoon turmeric powder
1 cup (250 ml) coconut milk
Juice of 1 lemon

Season the fish fillets with salt and pepper.

Heat the oil until hot in a large frying pan and sear the fillets to firm the flesh, then set aside.

Reheat the oil and add the diced onion (not the onion rings), curry leaves, garlic, green chillies, cardamom pods, fenugreek and lemongrass. Stir-fry over medium heat until fragrant.

Add the coriander, cumin and turmeric, and stir-fry until the aromas are released. Add the coconut milk and bring to a boil. Lower the heat and add the onion rings and fish fillets. Simmer until the fish fillets are tender, about 15 minutes, adding water if the mixture is too dry. Remove from the heat. Cool slightly and add the lemon juice to taste.

Portuguese Fishball Curry

A very tasty dish of spiced fishballs which are slowly simmered in a tempting curry gravy.

700 g (1½ lbs) fresh fish fillets,
    pulsed in a blender to yield
    2 cups minced fish
100 g (½ cup) finely chopped onion
3 cloves garlic, minced
1–2 green finger-length chillies, minced
2 egg whites
4 cups (1 litre) coconut milk
1 teaspoon Roasted Curry Powder
    (page 29) or fish curry powder
1–2 teaspoons chilli powder
1 teaspoon turmeric powder
1 sprig curry leaves
Juice of 1 lime
Salt and pepper, to taste

Place the minced fish in a bowl. Add ½ of the onion, garlic and green chilli, and mix well with the egg white. Shape the mixture into balls about 4 cm (1½ in) in diameter.

In a large pan, combine the coconut milk, curry powder, chilli powder, turmeric powder, curry leaves and the remaining onion, garlic and green chilli. Bring to a boil, then reduce the heat. Add the fishballs, cover and cook, stirring occasionally, until the fish balls are tender, about 10 minutes.

Deep-fried Battered Fish

500 g (1 lb) baby sardines or
    whitebait
Salt, to taste
Pinch of ground pepper
Juice of 2 limes
3 tablespoons rice flour
Oil, for deep-frying

Clean and wash the fish well.

Marinate the fish with the salt,
pepper and lime juice. Coat the fish
in the flour and deep-fry in hot oil
until tender but not too crispy.

Tamarind Claypot Fish

The southwestern coastal town
of Ambalangoda first made this
dish famous. A classic example of
claypot cookery, the tamarind both
imparts its characteristic sharp taste
and also acts as a preservative. Even
in Sri Lanka's heat and humidity,
an *ambulthiyal* can keep for up to
a week. Serve with plain rice.

1 tablespoon dried tamarind pulp
    soaked in 4 tablespoons water
500 g (1 lb) fresh tuna or other firm fish
Juice of 1 lime
4 teaspoons chilli powder
1 teaspoon ground pepper
Salt, to taste
6 cloves
1 slice fresh ginger
5 cloves garlic
1 sprig curry leaves
½ cup (125 ml) water

Soak the tamarind pulp in 4 tablespoons
of water, mash, stir and strain to obtain
the juice, discarding any solids.

Cut the fish into eight pieces, wash them
well with the lime juice and arrange the
pieces in a single layer in a pan.

Blend the tamarind juice, chilli powder,
pepper, salt and a little water to a paste.
Mix this paste with the fish in the pan,
coating each piece thoroughly. Add the
cloves, ginger, garlic, curry leaves and
the water, and bring to a boil. Simmer
until all the gravy has reduced and
the fish pieces are quite dry, about
15 minutes.

Deep-fried Battered Fish (top left)
and Tamarind Claypot Fish (right).

Prawns in a Coconut Curry Gravy

2 tablespoons oil
100 g (¾ cup) minced onion
6–7 cloves garlic, chopped
1 tablespoon minced fresh ginger
1 sprig curry leaves
1 cinnamon stick
1–2 green finger-length chillies
1 teaspoon chilli powder
1 teaspoon turmeric powder
4 teaspoons Roasted Curry Powder
   (page 29) or fish curry powder
1 large tomato, diced
Salt, to taste
700 g (1½ lbs) fresh medium prawns,
   peeled and deveined
1½ cups (375 ml) thick coconut milk

Heat the oil in a pan and fry the onion, garlic, ginger, curry leaves, cinnamon and green chillies until the onion is golden brown.

Add the chilli powder, turmeric and curry powder, diced tomato and salt. Cook, stirring frequently, until the tomato is fully mashed, about 10 minutes.

Add the prawns and simmer until cooked, about 3 minutes. Pour in the thick coconut milk and bring to a boil again. Remove from the heat and serve.

Stir-fried Spicy Prawns

700 g (1½ lbs) fresh medium prawns,
    peeled and deveined
Salt, to taste
2 teaspoons coarsely pounded red chillies
1 teaspoon turmeric powder
1 teaspoon lime juice
1–2 teaspoons oil
200 g (1 cup) sliced onion
5 cloves garlic, sliced
1–2 green finger-length chillies, sliced
1 small cinnamon stick
1 teaspoon crushed peppercorns
1 small tomato, cut in wedges
1 sprig curry leaves

Rub the prawns with the salt, pounded red chillies, turmeric powder and lime juice, and allow to marinate for 20 minutes.

Heat the oil in a pan and quickly stir-fry the prawns at high heat until half done, about 2 minutes. Remove from the pan and set aside.

In the same pan, fry the onions, garlic, green chillies, cinnamon, pepper, tomato wedges and curry leaves until crispy, about 3 minutes.

Return the prawns to the pan and toss to coat the prawns completely. Cook for 3 minutes or until done.

Curried Prawns

100 g (1 cup) diced onion
2–3 green finger-length chillies, diced
¼ tablespoon turmeric powder
1 tablespoon Unroasted Curry Powder (page 29) or fish curry powder
1 tablespoon chilli powder
10 cm (4 in) pandanus leaf
1 sprig curry leaves
1 cinnamon stick
700 g (1½ lbs) fresh jumbo prawns, peeled and deveined
½ cup (125 ml) thin coconut milk
½ tablespoon mustard powder
½ cup (125 ml) thick coconut milk
½ teaspoon chopped cabbage leaves (or any other leafy vegetable)
Juice of 1 lime
Salt, to taste

In a large pan, mix the onions, chillies, turmeric powder, curry powder, chilli powder, pandanus leaf, curry leaves, cinnamon and prawns. Add the thin coconut milk and mustard powder, bring to a boil and simmer for 5 to 8 minutes.

Add the thick coconut milk, return to a boil and simmer until the ingredients are tender, about 5 minutes. Add the cabbage leaves and remove from the heat. Season with lime juice and salt to taste.

Curried Squid

500 g (1 lb) fresh small squid, including heads
2 teaspoons oil
1 small onion, chopped
1 sprig curry leaves
1 cinnamon stick
3 green finger-length chillies, chopped
1 teaspoon chopped garlic
½ teaspoon chopped fresh ginger
1½ teaspoons Unroasted Curry Powder (page 29) or fish curry powder
Pinch of turmeric powder
Pinch of chilli powder
1 small tomato, chopped
Salt and pepper, to taste
½ cup (125 ml) thin coconut milk
½ cup (125 ml) thick coconut milk

Clean, wash the squid and remove the heads. Stuff each head into the body of each squid.

Heat the oil and stir-fry the onions, curry leaves, cinnamon and green chillies, about 5 minutes.

Add the garlic, ginger, curry powder, turmeric and chilli powder, and cook for another 5 minutes.

Add the chopped tomatoes, and season with salt and pepper. Add the squid and thin coconut milk, bring to a boil and simmer. When the liquid is reduced by half, add the thick coconut milk, return to a boil and cook until done, about 5 minutes.

Curried Prawns (bottom) and Curried Squid (top right).

Vadai Prawn Patties

Vadais are among the most popular snack foods in Sri Lanka. They are sold fresh and hot from street hawkers who patrol neighbourhoods with their entire kitchen on the front of a bicycle, at cricket matches, in any fast-food restaurant—even on the trains by men who shuffle down the aisle hailing their wares in a staccato, "Wadi, wadi!"

500 g (2 cups) masoor (Mysore) dhal
1 green finger-length chilli, chopped
2–3 dried red finger-length chillies, chopped
2 medium onions, chopped
1 sprig curry leaves
3½ tablespoons Maldive fish, or dried prawns/fish, chopped
Salt and pepper, to taste
20 fresh large prawns, peeled and deveined, with tails intact
Oil, for deep-fryings

Wash the dhal and pick it over carefully to remove any stones. Soak for 3 hours, then drain (reserving the water), and grind to a fine paste in a blender, adding a little of the reserved water if necessary. Add the green and red chillies, onion, curry leaves, Maldive fish or dried prawns, salt and pepper. Blend well.

Shape the blended mixture into patties, 5 cm (2 in) in diameter and 12 mm (½ in) thick, so that the patties resemble thick spectacle lenses. Each patty is called a vadai. Carefully press a prawn into the middle of each vadai until the prawn is firmly embedded. Heat the oil until hot and deep-fry the vadais to a golden brown. Remove with a slotted spoon, drain on kitchen towel and serve. Makes about 50 vadais.

Coconut Curry Crabs

Sri Lankan crab is famous throughout the region. Fresh crabs, so plentiful in the seas here, are simmered to perfection in a spiced coconut curry gravy.

3 kg (6½ lbs) fresh crabs
1 onion, sliced
2 green finger-length chillies,
 chopped
3½ tablespoons Roasted Curry
 Powder (page 29) or fish
 curry powder
2 teaspoons turmeric powder
½ teaspoon chilli powder
1 teaspoon fenugreek
 powder

2 teaspoons dried tamarind
 pulp, soaked in 2 table-
 spoons water, mashed and
 strained to obtain the juice
1 sprig curry leaves
2 cups (500 ml) water
4 cups (1 litre) thick coconut
 milk
½ teaspoon mustard powder
Juice of 1 lime
Salt and pepper, to taste

Clean the crabs, removing the carapace and splitting them into quarters with a cleaver. Place in a large pan, add all the other ingredients except the coconut milk, mustard powder, lime juice and salt. Bring to a boil then add the coconut milk, return the mixture to simmering point, and simmer gently for 20 minutes. Add the mustard powder, lime juice, salt and pepper, and stir for a few minutes until the flavours are married.

Remove from the heat and serve hot.

Meat & Poultry Dishes

Chicken Curry

This is a main course dish best served with vegetable curries, sambols and condiments as accompaniments.

2 teaspoons chilli powder
3 teaspoons fennel powder
2 teaspoons coriander powder
1 chicken (about 1 kg/2 lbs),
    cut into 8 pieces
1 teaspoon salt, or to taste
2 tablespoons vinegar
2 tablespoons oil
1 small onion, chopped
50 g (¼ cup) chopped garlic
½ teaspoon chopped fresh ginger
1 sprig curry leaves
1 stalk lemongrass, tender inner
    part of bottom third only, bruised
1 small cinnamon stick
1 teaspoon mustard seeds
1 cup (250 ml) coconut milk

In a frying pan, dry-roast the chilli, fennel and coriander powders for 2 minutes, until aromatic. Coat the chicken pieces with the spices, add the salt and vinegar, and set aside for 30 minutes.

Heat the oil in a separate pan. Add the chopped onion, garlic, ginger, curry leaves, lemongrass, cinnamon and mustard seeds, and fry until the onion is soft and golden, and the mustard seeds pop. Add the chicken and gently stir-fry for 20 minutes. Add the coconut milk, bring to a boil and simmer until the chicken is tender, about 15 minutes. Toss occasionally so that the gravy covers the chicken with a thick, dry coating.

Chicken Curry (right) and Coconut and Cashew Nut Chicken (left).

Coconut and Cashew Nut Chicken

Simple to prepare, this Coconut and Cashew Nut Chicken tastes excellent with rice.

1 chicken (about 1 kg/2 lbs), cleaned and
    cut into 8 pieces
2 tablespoons oil
2 cups (500 ml) coconut milk
¼ cup (60 ml) warm water
1 teaspoon salt, or to taste

MARINADE
40 g (⅓ cup) dry-roasted unsalted cashew nuts
½ teaspoon uncooked long-grain rice,
    dry-roasted
4 teaspoons unsweetened desiccated coconut,
    dry-roasted
4 teaspoons water
1 teaspoon chilli powder, dry-roasted
2 teaspoons fennel powder
2 teaspoons cumin powder
50 g (¼ cup) sliced onion rings
50 g (¼ cup) sliced tomato
½ teaspoon fenugreek seeds
2 green finger-length chillies, roughly chopped
    or left whole and scored
1 short cinnamon stick
½ teaspoon chopped fresh ginger

To prepare the Marinade, grind the cashew nuts, rice, coconut and water in a blender until the mixture forms a fine paste. Mix this paste with the remaining Marinade ingredients. Thoroughly coat the chicken pieces with this Marinade and leave to marinate for at least 20 minutes.

Heat the oil in a pan until hot. Add the marinated chicken and stir-fry for 10 minutes. Add half of the coconut milk diluted with the warm water, and salt. Bring to a boil, cover and simmer for 10 minutes. Add the rest of the coconut milk and simmer, uncovered, until the mix becomes a thick gravy, about 15 minutes.

Curried Meatballs

700 g (1½ lbs) minced beef
1 teaspoon salt
100 g (½ cup) chopped onion
½ green finger-length chilli, chopped
2 tablespoons oil, for stir-frying
2 tablespoons chopped garlic
½ teaspoon chopped fresh ginger
6–8 curry leaves

½ stalk lemongrass, tender inner part of bottom third only, bruised
1 teaspoon chilli powder
1 teaspoon fennel powder
1 teaspoon coriander powder
½ teaspoon turmeric powder
2 tablespoons dried tamarind pulp
1 cup (250 ml) coconut milk
1 teaspoon salt, or to taste

Mix the minced beef with the salt, ½ teaspoon chopped onion and green chilli. Using moistened hands, form the mixture into small balls.

Heat the oil to medium hot in a frying pan and add the remaining onion, garlic, ginger, curry leaves and lemongrass. Fry until brown.

Add all the powdered spices and fry for another 3 minutes. Add the tamarind pulp, coconut milk and salt, and bring to a boil. Add the meat balls, lower the heat and simmer for another 10 minutes.

Clockwise from top: Spicy Stir-fried Lamb, pappadams, Bird's-eye Chilli Sambol and freshly grated coconut

Spicy Stir-fried Lamb

Lamb, venison, wild boar, hare and game birds have always played an important role in Sri Lankan cuisine. In this recipe, lamb is stir-fried with spices, sour belimbi and vinegar to produce a hot, dry curry that goes equally well with plain rice or breads.

2 tablespoons oil
2 tablespoons chopped
    onion
10 cm (4 in) pandanus leaf
1 sprig curry leaves
1 cinnamon stick
700 g (1½ lbs) lamb, cut
    into 4-cm (1½-in) slices
1 teaspoon turmeric
    powder
Salt, to taste
3 cloves garlic, chopped

1 teaspoon chopped fresh
    ginger
2 tablespoons dried
    belimbi or 1 tablespoon
    dried tamarind pulp
2 tablespoons vinegar
1 tablespoon crushed
    black peppercorns
1 small onion, quartered
10 green finger-length
    chillies, halved
    lengthwise

Heat the oil in a frying pan until medium hot and add the chopped onion, pandanus leaf, curry leaves and cinnamon. Fry until the onions turn golden brown.

Add the lamb, turmeric and salt, and cook over low heat, about 10 minutes. Add the garlic, ginger and belimbi or tamarind pulp. Cook for a further 15 minutes depending on the size of the venison pieces (allow slightly longer for larger pieces). Add the vinegar, crushed peppercorns, quartered onions and chillies. Remove from the heat when the chillies and onions are half-cooked, about 5 minutes.

Lamb Curry

2 tablespoons oil
1 onion, chopped
5 cloves garlic, chopped
2.5 cm (1 in) fresh ginger, chopped
2 green finger-length chillies,
    chopped
1 stalk lemongrass, tender inner part
    of bottom third only
½ small cinnamon stick
2–3 cardamom pods, smashed in a
    mortar
700 g (1½ lbs) boneless lamb, cubed
2 tablespoons Roasted Curry Powder
    (page 29) or meat curry powder
1 teaspoon chilli powder
2 teaspoons turmeric powder
1 teaspoon ground black pepper
2 large tomatoes, diced
¾ cup (200 ml) thick coconut milk
Salt, to taste

Heat the oil in a pan and stir-fry the
onion, garlic, ginger, green chillies,
lemongrass, cinnamon and cardamons
until the onion is golden brown.

Add the lamb and stir well to coat,
then add the curry powder, chilli
and turmeric powders, pepper and
tomatoes. Cook over medium heat
until the meat becomes tender, about
40 minutes. Add the thick coconut
milk, bring to a boil and simmer a few
minutes longer, adjust the seasoning,
and serve.

Pork Curry

2 tablespoons oil
1 onion, chopped
5 cloves garlic, chopped
2.5 cm (1 in) fresh ginger, chopped
1 stalk lemongrass, tender inner part
    of bottom third only, chopped
700 g (1½ lbs) boneless pork, cubed
2 teaspoons dried tamarind pulp,
    soaked in 2 tablespoons water,
    mashed and strained to obtain
    the juice
1¾ cups (400 ml) water
2 sprigs curry leaves
4 teaspoons Roasted Curry Powder
    (page 29) or meat curry powder
1 teaspoon crushed black
    peppercorns
2–3 cloves
½ small cinnamon stick
Salt, to taste

Heat the oil in a pan and stir-fry the
onion, garlic, ginger and lemongrass
until the onion is golden brown.

Add all the remaining ingredients and
bring to a boil. Reduce the heat and
simmer uncovered until the gravy is
thick and the pork tender, about 25
minutes.

Lamb Curry (above) and Pork Curry
(below right).

Royal Chicken

Once, this dish would only have graced the King of Kandy's table. Today it is a tasty, if less lofty, main course dish best served with vegetable curries, sambols and condiments as accompaniments.

2 tablespoons oil
1 small onion, chopped
1 sprig curry leaves
5 cm (2 in) pandanus leaf
1 short cinnamon stick
3 cloves
3 cardamom pods
1 teaspoon minced garlic
1 teaspoon minced fresh ginger
1 teaspoon cumin powder
2 teaspoons coriander powder
½ teaspoon fennel powder
Pinch of turmeric powder
1 chicken (1 kg/2 lbs), cut into 8 pieces
2 cups (500 ml) thin coconut milk
½ teaspoon tamarind juice (page 27)
½ cup (125 ml) thick coconut milk
½ teaspoon mustard seeds
3–4 dill seeds
1½ teaspoons salt, or to taste
½ teaspoon ground pepper
1–2 green and/or red finger-length chillies, sliced (optional)

Heat the oil until medium hot, add the onion, curry leaves, pandanus leaf, cinnamon, cloves, cardamoms, garlic and ginger, and fry for 2 to 3 minutes. Stir in the cumin, coriander, fennel and turmeric, and fry for a further 30 seconds then add the chicken and cook, turning the chicken pieces, until the meat is brown on all sides.

Add the thin coconut milk, bring to a boil and simmer for 10 minutes. Mix the tamarind juice with the thick coconut milk, add to the curry. Return to a boil and simmer for 12 minutes.

Meanwhile, in a separate pan, heat more oil and roast the mustard and dill seeds, then cool and grind to a powder in a blender. When the chicken is tender, add the ground mustard and dill mix, salt and pepper, and stir well. Remove from the heat and garnish with sliced chillies, if desired. Serve as a main dish with rice and accompaniments.

Beef Smore

A dish of Dutch origin. In Sri Lanka, beef smore is a real treat—a whole beef fillet or loin which is slowly simmered in a spicy coconut milk gravy and then sliced and served in its own gravy. Eat with rice or breads of your choice.

700 g (1½ lbs) beef sirloin
2 tablespoons white vinegar
Salt and pepper, or to taste
2 tablespoons ghee or oil for
    stir-frying
2 sprigs curry leaves
1 stalk lemongrass, tender inner
    part of bottom third only,
    finely sliced
1 onion, sliced
1–2 green finger-length chillies,
    deseeded and finely sliced
½ teaspoon chilli powder
1 cup (250 ml) coconut milk

Pierce the beef all over with a fork or skewer and marinate in the vinegar, salt and pepper for 2 to 4 hours.

Heat the ghee or oil until very hot and sear the beef until lightly browned on all sides. This seals the meat and helps to retain the juices. Remove the meat from the pan and set aside.

To the same pan add the curry leaves, lemongrass, sliced onion and green chillies. Fry until half cooked, about 3 minutes. Add the chilli powder and mix well. Return the beef to the pan and add the coconut milk. Stir well and simmer until the coconut milk reduces into a thick gravy and the meat is done to your liking, about 25–35 minutes.

Remove from the heat, slice the meat to the desired thickness and pour the gravy over the slices.

Vegetable Dishes

Spicy Eggplant

The eggplants in Sri Lanka are tiny round pea eggplants, which may not be readily available elsewhere. Any other type of eggplant may be used, although the taste will be different.

2 large Asian eggplants
   (about 500 g / 1 lb total)
½ cup (125 ml) oil
1 medium onion, sliced
5 cm (2 in) pandanus leaf
1 sprig curry leaves
1 small cinnamon stick
½ teaspoon sliced green finger-length chillies
½ teaspoon ground Maldive fish or dried prawns
4 tablespoons coconut milk or water
½ teaspoon dried red chilli flakes
Salt, to taste
3 tablespoons lime juice

Wash the eggplants then crush them with a spoon if using tiny pea eggplants. If using other types of eggplant, cut it into small dice. Fry in the hot oil until they lose their firmness.

In another pan, heat 2 tablespoons of oil and stir-fry the onion, pandanus leaf, curry leaves, cinnamon and chillies for several minutes until the onion is golden brown. Add the Maldive fish or dried prawns, coconut milk or water, chilli flakes and salt, and cook over medium heat for 5 minutes. Add the fried eggplants and lime juice, and season to taste. Serve hot as an accompaniment to other dishes.

Dhal Stew

250 g (1¼ cups) channa dhal or yellow split peas
2 teaspoons oil
1 medium onion, sliced
½ teaspoon chopped garlic
1 sprig curry leaves
2–3 dried finger-length chillies, roughly chopped
5 cm (2 in) pandanus leaf
1 teaspoon mustard seeds, whole
1 teaspoon curry powder
1 teaspoon turmeric powder
1 tablespoon Maldive fish or dried prawns
½ teaspoon fenugreek seeds
5 cups (1.25 litres) thin coconut milk
¾ cup (200 ml) thick coconut milk
1 teaspoon salt

Wash and soak the dhal in water for 30 minutes, then drain.

Heat the oil in a pan and stir-fry the onion, garlic, curry leaves, chilli and pandanus leaf until the onions are soft. Add the mustard seeds and fry for a few seconds until the seeds pop. Add the dhal, curry powder, turmeric powder, Maldive fish or dried prawns, fenugreek and thin coconut milk. Bring to a boil and simmer until the dhal is tender, about 25 minutes. Add the thick coconut milk and salt. Simmer for a few more minutes while stirring. Remove from the heat and serve hot as an accompaniment to other dishes.

Dhal Stew (above) and Curried Cabbage (below).

Curried Cabbage

500 g (1 lb) cabbage
100 g (½ cup) chopped onions
1 tablespoons chopped garlic
2–3 green finger-length chillies, chopped
1 teaspoon crushed peppercorns
½ teaspoon turmeric powder
2 teaspoons Unroasted Curry Powder (page 29) or regular curry powder
½ teaspoon fenugreek seeds
½ teaspoon Maldive fish or dried prawns
1 small cinnamon stick
1⅔ cups (400 ml) thin coconut milk
¾ cup (200 ml) thick coconut milk
1½ teaspoons salt

Cut the cabbage into large strips, and wash thoroughly. Set aside.

Place the onion, garlic, chillies, peppercorns, turmeric powder, curry powder, fenugreek, Maldive fish or dried prawns, cinnamon and thin coconut milk into a pan. Cook over low heat until the seeds are tender, about 15 minutes. Add the cabbage and thick coconut milk, bring to a boil and simmer for 5 minutes. Remove from the heat and serve hot as an accompaniment to other dishes.

Curried Okra

500 g (1 lb) okra (ladies' fingers),
   washed, tops removed, cut into
   thick diagonal slices
Pinch of turmeric powder
Oil, for deep-frying
2 tablespoons chopped onion
1 sprig curry leaves
1 teaspoon curry powder
1 teaspoon ground Maldive fish
   or dried prawns
1 cinnamon stick
1 teaspoon dill seeds
Salt, to taste
2 teaspoons lime juice
1½ cups (375 ml) coconut milk

Rub the okra with the turmeric
powder (be careful as turmeric
stains the fingers). Heat the oil and
deep-fry the okra until light brown,
then remove from the oil with a
strainer and set aside to drain.

Place the rest of the ingredients
in a pan and bring to a boil.
Reduce the heat and simmer until
the onions are cooked, about 10
minutes.

Add the deep-fried okra, continue
to simmer for another 5 minutes.
Remove from the heat and serve.

Curried Okra (left) and
Spicy Green Beans (right).

Spicy Green Beans

500 g (1 lb) green beans, cut into
    4-cm (1½-in) lengths
Oil, for deep-frying
1 onion, finely chopped
5 cm (2 in) pandanus leaf
1 sprig curry leaves
1 small cinnamon stick
3 green finger-length chillies,
    finely chopped
Pinch of turmeric powder
2 teaspoons Roasted Curry
    Powder (see page 29) or regular
    curry powder
½ teaspoon ground black pepper
½ cup (125 ml) thin coconut milk
½ cup (125 ml) thick coconut milk
3 tablespoons lime juice
Salt, to taste

Deep-fry the green beans in very
hot oil for 3 minutes, then remove
the beans from the oil with a
strainer and set aside to drain.

Reheat 2 tablespoons of the oil
in a separate pan and stir-fry
the onion, pandanus leaf, curry
leaves, cinnamon and green
chillies, until the onions are soft.
Add the turmeric powder, curry
powder, pepper and thin coconut
milk, and simmer for about 5
minutes. Add the thick coconut
milk and green beans, season with
lime juice and salt, and simmer
until the remaining coconut milk
evaporates.

Tangy Coconut Okra

500 g (1 lb) okra (ladies' fingers),
    washed, tops removed, cut into
    thick diagonal slices
Oil, for frying
1 medium onion, chopped
1 teaspoon cumin seeds
1 sprig curry leaves
1 teaspoon turmeric powder
1 green finger-length chilli, slit in half
    and deseeded
½ teaspoon fenugreek seeds
1–2 tablespoons chilli powder
¼ cup (60 ml) tamarind juice (page 27)
⅓ cup (100 ml) thick coconut milk
1 teaspoon salt, or to taste

Deep-fry the okra in very hot oil until
light brown, remove the okra with a
strainer and set aside to drain.

Spoon 1 or 2 tablespoons of the oil
into a pan and add all the remaining
ingredients except the okra, tamarind
juice, coconut milk and salt. Stir-fry for
10 minutes over medium heat.

Add the tamarind juice and cook for a
further 10 minutes over low heat. Add
the okra, coconut milk and salt, bring
to a boil and simmer for 10 minutes.
Remove from the heat and serve hot as
an accompaniment to other dishes.

Portuguese Omelette

4 eggs
1 green finger-length chilli,
    chopped
1 small onion, chopped
¼ cup (50 g) chopped tomatoes
1 tablespoon oil

GRAVY
1 tablespoon curry powder
1 tablespoon chilli powder
½ sprig curry leaves
½ teaspoon turmeric powder
½ small cinnamon stick
½ teaspoon fenugreek seeds
½ tablespoon ground Maldive fish
    or dried prawns
2 cups (500 ml) thick coconut milk
½ teaspoon salt, or to taste

Beat the eggs in a bowl. Add the
green chillies, onion and tomatoes.

Heat the oil in a frying pan and
pour in the egg mixture to make an
omelette. When set, remove from
the heat and cut into large pieces.

To make the Gravy, place all the
ingredients in a pan and bring to a
boil. Reduce the heat, and simmer
for 5 minutes. Season to taste
before serving over the omelette.

Tangy Coconut Okra (left) and
Portuguese Omelette (top right).

Green Mango Curry

This classical Sinhalese dish can be traced back to the fifth century, when it was served at the court of King Kasyapa of Sigiriya.

1 tablespoon oil
1 onion, chopped
6 cloves garlic, chopped
1½ teaspoons chopped fresh ginger
2 sprigs curry leaves
1 red finger-length chilli, sliced
4 teaspoons Roasted Curry Powder
    (page 29) or regular curry powder
½ small cinnamon stick
1 teaspoon salt, or to taste
700 g (1½ lbs) green mangoes, peeled and
    pitted, flesh cut into long, thick strips
Scant ½ cup (100 ml) thin coconut milk
1 teaspoon mustard powder
3 tablespoons vinegar
¾ cup (200 ml) thick coconut milk
1 tablespoon sugar

Heat the oil in a pan and stir-fry the onion, garlic, ginger, curry leaves and red chillies until the onion is soft.

Add the curry powder, cinnamon, salt, mango and thin coconut milk. Bring to a boil and simmer until the mango is just tender, about 10 minutes.

Meanwhile, mix the mustard powder with a little vinegar to form a paste. Stir the mustard paste into the thick coconut milk and, when the mango is tender, add the mustard and thick coconut milk, and the sugar to the curry.

Bring to a boil, reduce the heat and simmer for about 5 minutes. Adjust the seasoning. The gravy should be thick enough to thoroughly coat the mango.

Pumpkin Curry

700 g (1½ lbs) pumpkin, peeled, washed and cut into medium chunks
100 g (½ cup) chopped onion
1–2 green finger-length chillies, chopped
4 cloves garlic, chopped
5 cm (2 in) pandanus leaf
1 sprig curry leaves
1 teaspoon turmeric powder
½ teaspoon chilli powder
2 teaspoons Roasted Curry Powder (page 29) or regular curry powder

1½ teaspoons salt, or to taste
2 cups (500 ml) thin coconut milk
2 tablespoons uncooked rice mixed with 2 tablespoons freshly grated coconut, dry-roasted until golden brown and then ground in a blender to yield 2 tablespoons
1 cup (250 ml) thick coconut milk

Place all the ingredients except the ground coconut-rice mixture and thick coconut milk into a pan, bring to a boil, reduce the heat and simmer until the pumpkin is almost tender, about 15 minutes.

Dissolve the ground coconut-rice mixture into the thick coconut milk. Add to the simmering curry and cook over low heat until the gravy is thick and coats the pumpkin pieces, about 5 to 10 minutes.

Desserts & Drinks

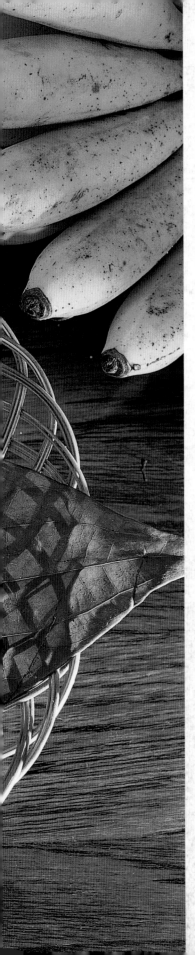

Topknot Cakes

These deep-fried cakes, sporting a topknot, are a popular snack or dessert.

500 g (4 cups) rice flour
2 cups (500 ml) brown syrup or
    maple syrup
Oil, for deep-frying

Using a fine sieve, sift the rice flour into a large mixing bowl and add the syrup. (If the mixture is too thick add a little hot water.) Set aside for 30 minutes.

Heat the oil to low temperature, about 150°C (300°F). Pour the mixture, about ¼ cup (60 ml), at a time into the hot oil. After a few minutes the cakes will begin to stiffen. Insert a sharp-tipped wooden skewer or satay stick into the centre of each cake and turn it in one direction while slowly lifting the batter out of the pan. The uncooked batter will emerge looking like a cookie with a topknot. When each cake reaches a dark brown colour, remove from the oil and set aside to drain on paper towels to remove excess oil. Makes about 30 pieces.

Coconut Cakes

2 cups (500 ml) brown syrup or
    maple syrup
500 g (5 cups) freshly grated
    coconut
250 g (1¼ cups) dried mung beans,
    dry-roasted
½ teaspoon salt
200 g (1½ cups) rice flour
Oil, for deep-frying

Heat the syrup to simmering point and add the grated coconut. Stir continuously for 10 minutes then remove from the heat and set aside.

Coarsely grind the mung beans in a blender to obtain a flour. Combine the ground mung beans with the syrup and mix into a paste. Shape the paste into 2.5-cm (1-in) round balls using the palms of the hands. Roll the balls on the rice flour until it coats them well. Heat the oil and deep-fry the balls until golden brown. Makes about 30 pieces.

Topknot cakes

Coconut Cinnamon Cashew Slices

350 g (1¾ cups) sugar
700 g (7 cups) unsweetened
   desiccated coconut
2 teaspoons cinnamon powder
¼ teaspoon clove powder
200 g (1⅔ cups) raw cashew nuts,
   dry-roasted and chopped in a
   food processor
Pinch of salt

Place the sugar in a pan. Heat while stirring continuously until the sugar melts and begins to thicken. Add the coconut, cinnamon and clove powder. Stir the mixture until it pulls away from the sides of the pan. Add the cashew nuts and stir well. Remove from the heat.

Oil a baking tray, or stainless steel or wooden table top, and roll the hot nut mixture into a thin layer about 2 cm (¾ in) thick. Cut into 2.5-cm (1-in) squares and allow to cool.

Cashew Brittle (third row from left) and Coconut Cinnamon Cashew Slices in three colours.

Cashew Brittle

1 kg (2 lbs) raw cashew nuts
500 g (2½ cups) sugar

Roast the cashew nuts in a slow
oven (150°C/300°F) until golden
brown. Remove from the oven and
cool. Crush the nuts into small, even
chunks using a rolling pin.

Caramelise the sugar in a frying pan.
Stir in the nuts with a spatula. Oil
a baking tray, or stainless steel, or
wooden table top and roll the hot
nut mixture into a thin layer about
12 mm (½ in) thick. Cut into 2.5-cm
(1-in) squares and allow to cool.

Coconut Spice Cake

This dessert hails from the kitchens of the Portuguese colonial era.

500 g (1 lb) jaggery (substitute shaved palm sugar or dark brown sugar)
250 g (1¼ cups) fine granulated sugar
¾ cup (200 ml) coconut milk
¼ teaspoon salt, or to taste
500 g (1 lb) freshly grated coconut
50 g (⅓ cup) plain (all-purpose) flour
100 g (¾ cup) chopped cashew nuts
1 teaspoon mixed clove, cardamon and cinnamon powder
1 teaspoon grated lemon zest

Preheat the oven to 160°C (325°F).

Dissolve the jaggery (or palm sugar) and granulated sugar in the coconut milk. Place this liquid into a pan, add the salt and bring to a boil. Add the grated coconut and cook until the mixture is sticky but not burnt.

Remove from the heat and slowly stir in the flour, mixing well. Stir in the cashew nuts and mixed spices. Add the lemon zest and pour into a 23 cm x 30 cm (9 in x 12 in) pan.

Bake in the preheated oven until done, about 30 minutes. The cake will be done when a toothpick pushed into the centre has no batter sticking to it as it is withdrawn. Cool and cut into slices.

Sweet Coconut Slices

This jouncy jellied sweetmeat is a specialty of the region southward from the Buddhist pilgrimage town of Kalutara some 30 km (20 miles) south of Colombo.

6 cups (1.5 litres) thick coconut milk
⅜ cup (100 ml) brown syrup or palm sugar syrup or maple syrup
250 g (8 oz) jaggery, finely grated (shaved palm sugar or dark brown sugar may be substituted)
¼ teaspoon salt, or to taste
250 g (2 cups) rice flour
50 g (⅓ cup) raw cashew nuts, broken into bits

Place the coconut milk in a bowl and add the syrup, jaggery and salt, and mix well. Strain.

Place the rice flour into a large pan and slowly pour in the coconut-jaggery mixture, mixing well. Add the cashew nuts and bring the mixture to a boil, stirring continuously with a large metal (not wooden) spoon until the mixture is bubbling. Spoon off any oil that rises to the top of the pan. Cook the mixture until it gets dark and pulls away off the sides of the pan in a sticky lump.

Remove from the heat and flatten into a baking tray and cover with waxed paper. Place in the refrigerator to cool and stiffen. It should then become quite rubbery. When cold, cut into pieces of desired size and serve.

Portuguese Semolina Love Cake

As the name implies, this dish is one of the culinary legacies of the Portuguese. Although it can be found throughout Sri Lanka, the origin of its name remains a mystery.

14 egg yolks
500 g (2 cups) soft brown sugar
350 g (1¾ cups) semolina flour, lightly dry-roasted
150 g (¾ cup) unsalted butter, softened
1 teaspoon rose essence or 1 tablespoon rose water
1 teaspoon vanilla essence
¼ cup (60 ml) honey
1 teaspoon cardamom powder
300 g (2 cups) finely chopped cashew nuts
4 egg whites
Pure icing (confectioner's) sugar

Preheat the oven to 150°C (300°F). Grease a 20-cm (8-in) square baking tin or other cake mould and line with several layers of waxed paper.

Beat the egg yolks and brown sugar until creamy. Mix the semolina flour with the softened butter and add to the egg yolk and sugar mixture, and beat until well mixed. Add the rose essence, vanilla essence, honey, cardamom powder and cashew nuts, and mix well.

Beat the egg whites until they form stiff peaks and fold into the mixture. Pour into the greased baking tin and bake for 1 to 1½ hours, until the top is browned and firm to touch. Remove from the oven and cool in the tin. Dust the top with icing (confectioner's) sugar.

HELPFUL HINT
If the top of the cake is turning brown too quickly during baking, cover with aluminium foil. For a crusted cake, sprinkle a thin layer of icing (confectioner's) sugar over the cake before baking.

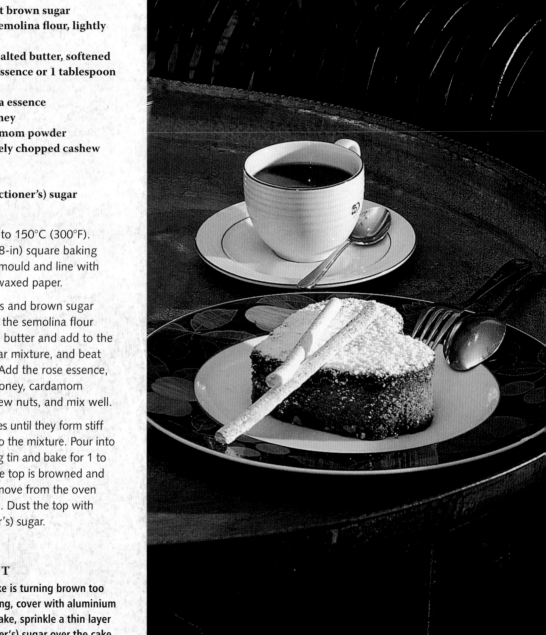

Coconut Halva

Halva originates from the Middle East but travelled east to India and Sri Lanka where it became a very popular snack or dessert item. Although the town of Negombo thirty kilometres north of Colombo is said to be the original "home" of halva, or *aluwa*, in Sri Lanka, today this grainy fudge is found just about everywhere on the island. *Aluwa* are traditionally cut into narrow diamond shapes.

400 g (3¼ cups) rice flour
100 g (½ cup) semolina flour
100 g (1 cup) freshly grated coconut
¾ cup (200 ml) brown syrup or palm sugar syrup or maple syrup
3 tablespoons water
1 teaspoon dry-roasted cumin seeds
½ teaspoon cardamom powder
3 tablespoons chopped raw cashew nuts
80 g (⅔ cup) raw cashew nuts, halved

Dry-roast the rice flour, semolina flour and grated coconut in a pan without burning. Boil the brown syrup or palm sugar syrup with a little water, remove from the heat and allow to cool slightly. Mix the rice flour mixture into the brown syrup. Add the cumin seeds, cardamom and chopped cashew nuts. Pour the mixture onto a baking tray lined with waxed paper, about 12 mm (½ in) in height. Dot the top with the cashew nut halves. Cut into narrow diamonds while still hot. Serve at room temperature.

Refreshing Orange Spice Cooler

500 g (2½ cups) sugar
12 cups (3 litres) water
2 cardamom pods
2 cloves
Juice of 4 oranges
Soaked *tulsi* (basil) seeds

Combine the sugar and water in a pot and bring to a boil with the cardamom and cloves. Simmer until reduced by a third.

Remove from the heat, discard the cardamoms and cloves then add the orange juice. Allow to cool to room temperature. Float some soaked *tulsi* (basil) seeds on top of the drink as a garnish then chill before serving.

Makes about 6 glasses.

LEFT TO RIGHT Iced Coffee (no recipe given), Refreshing Orange Spice Cooler, and Pineapple Cinnamon Cooler.

Pineapple Cinnamon Cooler

1 small pineapple (about 500 g/1 lb)
500 g (2½ cups) sugar
12 cups (3 litres) water
1 small cinnamon stick
3 tablespoons lime juice
Soaked *tulsi* (basil) seeds

Peel the pineapple, quarter it and remove the fibrous core. Extract the juice from the pineapple flesh with a food processor or juicer. Set aside.

Combine the sugar and water in a pot and bring to a boil with the cinnamon stick. Simmer until reduced by a third. Remove from the heat, discard the cinnamon stick then add the pineapple juice and lime juice. Allow to cool to room temperature.

Float some soaked *tulsi* seeds on top of the drink as a garnish then chill before serving.

Makes about 6 glasses.

Acknowledgements

The recipes in this book were created by the chefs at the following Sri Lankan hotels:

Heritance Kandalama Hotel
Tel: +94 66 555 5000
hkinfo@heritancehotels.com
heritancehotels.com
Chef Senaka Perera

Cinnamon Grand Colombo
Tel: +94 112 437 437
cinnamonhotels.freshdesk.com
cinnamonhotels.com/
cinnamongrandcolombo
Executive Sous Chef KMR Morugama
Chef Leo Perera
Chef HB Piyasena
Chef KDML Niranjan
Chef Kishore Reddy

Jetwing Lighthouse
Dadella, Galle
Tel: +94 912 223 744
resv.lighthouse@jetwinghotels.com
jetwinghotels.com
Executive Chef Mohan T Kulathunge

Mount Lavinia Hotel
Tel: +94 112 711 711
info@mountlaviniahotel.com
mountlaviniahotel.com
Chef Publis

Jetwing Blue
Negombo, Sri Lanka
Tel : +94 312 279 000
resv.blue@jetwinghotels.com
jetwinghotels.com/jetwingblue
Executive Chef Gamini Thambugala

Jetwing Yala
Tel: +94 47-4710 710
resv.yala@jetwinghotels.com
jetwinghotels.com/jetwingyala/#gref
Executive Chef Jayantha Ekanayake

SPECIAL THANKS

The publisher would like to thank Mount Lavinia Hotel, The Lanka Oberoi, Jetwing Hotels Ltd and Aitken Spence Hotel Management (Pvt) Ltd, for their generous support and assistance in producing this book.

Many individuals contributed recipes, information and assistance in preparing this book. We wish to thank Sanath Ukwatha, Bazeer Cassim and the staff of the Mount Lavinia Hotel; Ananda Yapa of the International Hotel School, Mount Lavinia for his endless patience explaining the fine points of Sri Lankan ingredients and to Philomena de Lanerolle for typing them up; Stefan Pfeiffer, Narmada L Müller and Chef Helmut Hubele of the Lanka Oberoi in Colombo; Hiran Cooray, Kumara Seneratne and Ruvinika Seneratne of Jetwing Hotels, Ltd.; Gemunu Goonewardene and S Amal Nanayakkara of Aitken Spence Hotel Management (Pvt) Ltd; Mrs Indra Rani Lavan Iswaran for her assistance in the selection of recipes; Mario de Alwis of Ma's Tropical Food Processing, Pvt Ltd; Ahsan Refai of Zam Gems and the staff of their shop at the Lanka Oberoi; Al-hajj MHA Gaffar and Al-hajj AG Kamal of the Historical Mansion in Galle; Lucky Perera of Lanka Hands for the use of backdrop items in the photos, Ms Deloraine Brohier and Graham de Kretser for their information about the Dutch Burgher cooking traditions; Nissanka Goonasekera of Giragala Village in Mirissa; Mr & Mrs Shanti Perera of Sunray Beach Villa in Mount Lavinia; Mrs. Tissa Warnasooriya and PP Hettiarachchi of the Ceylon Tourist Board; George Michael of the Ministry of Tourism; and Lawrence Wheeler. Thanks also to Chefs Kishore Reddy and Jayantha Ekanayake for reading the manuscript and suggesting improvements.

MAIL-ORDER INGREDIENTS

Most of the ingredients used in this book can be found in markets featuring the foods of Sri Lanka and India, as well as in other Asian foodstores and large supermarkets. Ingredients not found locally may be available from the mail-order markets listed below.

USA
Grocery Lanka Store
Tel: (301) 603 2191
support@grocerylanka.com
grocerylanka.com

Penzey's Spices
Tel: (800) 741 7787
Fax: (414) 760 7317
customerservice@penzeys.com
penzeys.com

Sri Lankan Delight
Tel: (818) 774 12137
info@lankandelight.com
lankandelight.com

The Spice House
Tel: (312) 676-2414
support@thespicehouse.com
thespicehouse.com

EUROPE
Bristol Sweet Mart
Tel: +44 117 9510 690
sales@sweetmart.co.uk
sweetmart.co.uk

Taj Stores
Tel: +44 01273 724571
info@taj.co.uk
tajstores.co.uk

AUSTRALIA
Manny's House of Spices
Tel: (02) 46485808
info@mannyspices.com.au
www.mannyspices.com.au

Index

"Books to Span the East and West"

Tuttle Publishing was founded in 1832 in the small New England town of Rutland, Vermont [USA]. Our core values remain as strong today as they were then—to publish best-in-class books which bring people together one page at a time. In 1948, we established a publishing office in Japan—and Tuttle is now a leader in publishing English-language books about the arts, languages and cultures of Asia. The world has become a much smaller place today and Asia's economic and cultural influence has grown. Yet the need for meaningful dialogue and information about this diverse region has never been greater. Over the past seven decades, Tuttle has published thousands of books on subjects ranging from martial arts and paper crafts to language learning and literature—and our talented authors, illustrators, designers and photographers have won many prestigious awards. We welcome you to explore the wealth of information available on Asia at **www.tuttlepublishing.com.**

Published by Tuttle Publishing, an imprint of Periplus Editions (HK) Ltd.

www.tuttlepublishing.com

Copyright © 2022 Periplus Editions (HK) Ltd.

ISBN 978-0-8048-5573-0
(*previously published* as ISBN 978-0-8048-4416-1 pb)

Photo credits
All food and location photography by Luca Invernizzi Tettoni. Additional photos on page 1, 6, 9, 10 and 12 by Dominic Sansoni.
Front endpapers: aksenovden/Shutterstock.com (photo ID 1084348016). Back endpapers: Aleksandar Kamasi/Shutterstock.com (photo ID 476456257).

Distributed by

North America, Latin America & Europe
Tuttle Publishing
364 Innovation Drive, North Clarendon
VT 05759-9436 U.S.A.
Tel: 1 (802) 773-8930; Fax: 1 (802) 773-6993
info@tuttlepublishing.com
www.tuttlepublishing.com

Asia Pacific
Berkeley Books Pte Ltd, 3 Kallang Sector #04-01, Singapore 349278.
Tel: (65) 6741-2178; Fax: (65) 6741-2179
inquiries@periplus.com.sg
www.tuttlepublishing.com

25 24 23 22   10 9 8 7 6 5 4 3 2 1

Printed in China   2206EP

TUTTLE PUBLISHING® is a registered trademark of Tuttle Publishing, a division of Periplus Editions (HK) Ltd.